ESCAPE ROOMS AND OTHER IMMERSIVE EXPERIENCES IN THE LIBRARY

ALA Editions purchases fund advocacy, awareness,
and accreditation programs for library professionals worldwide.

ESCAPE ROOMS AND OTHER IMMERSIVE EXPERIENCES IN THE LIBRARY

ELLYSSA KROSKI

CHICAGO 2019

ELLYSSA KROSKI is the Director of Information Technology at the New York Law Institute as well as an award-winning editor and author of thirty-seven books. She is a librarian, an adjunct faculty member at Drexel and San Jose State Universities, and an international conference speaker. She has just been named the winner of the 2017 Library Hi Tech Award from the ALA/LITA for her long-term contributions to library and information science technology and its application. She can be found at: http://amazon.com/author/ellyssa.

ISBNs
978-0-8389-1767-1 (paper)
978-0-8389-1790-9 (PDF)
978-0-8389-1789-3 (ePub)
978-0-8389-1791-6 (Kindle)

Library of Congress Cataloging-in-Publication Data

Names: Kroski, Ellyssa, author.
Title: Escape rooms and other immersive experiences in the library / Ellyssa Kroski.
Description: Chicago, IL : ALA Editions, an imprint of the American Library Association, 2019.
Identifiers: LCCN 2018025713 | ISBN 9780838917671 (print : alk. paper) | ISBN 9780838917893 (epub) | ISBN 9780838917909 (pdf) | ISBN 9780838917916 (kindle)
Subjects: LCSH: Libraries—Activity programs. | Group problem solving.
Classification: LCC Z716.33 .K764 2018 | DDC 025.5—dc23
LC record available at https://lccn.loc.gov/2018025713

Cover design by Krista Joy Johnson.

Text design in the Chaparral, Gotham, and Bell Gothic typefaces.

∞ This paper meets the requirements of ANSI/NISO Z39.48-1992 (Permanence of Paper).

Printed in the United States of America

23 22 21 20 19   5 4 3 2 1

Contents

List of Figures *vii*
Preface *ix*

PART I
Introducing Escape Rooms and Immersive Experiences

1 | Escape Rooms and Immersive Experiences Explained *3*

2 | The Escape Room Opportunity *23*

3 | Escape Room Activity in Libraries *35*

PART II
How to Create, Organize, and Run Eleven Project Types

4 | How to Host a Pre-Designed Escape Room Event *63*

5 | How to Design an Escape Room from Scratch *71*

6 | How to Create a Pop-up Escape Room *89*

7 | How to Create an Escape Room Enthusiasts Club *103*

8 | How to Host an Immersive Experience *111*

9 | How to Host a Kid-Friendly Escape Room Event *119*

10 | How to Design a Digital Breakout *125*

11 | All About Escape Room Board Games *133*

12 | How to Host an Escape Room Event for Team-Building and Staff Training *139*

13 | How to Add a High-Tech Twist to Your Escape Room *145*

14 | Start-to-Finish Model: *The Search for Alexander Hamilton and the Missing Librarian* *155*

APPENDIXES

A Escape Room Set-up Document Template *173*

B Escape Room Puzzle Document Template *175*

Resources *179*
Index *183*

Figures

1.1 Escape Thrill's *Wild West Room* 5

1.2 My mother and me with our gamemaster at Escape Countdown Tampa before our *Jailbreak* game 6

1.3 *An Evening in Paris* escape game designed for two at Escape Countdown Tampa 7

1.4 Three generations of my family about to play the *Legends of Atlantis* escape room at Backstage Escape Games, Myrtle Beach, South Carolina 8

1.5 The *Tragic Magic* game room at the Tampa Bay Escape Room 11

1.6 Augmented reality rare books exhibit titled the *Treasures and Technology of the New York Law Institute* immersed visitors in the library's collections 16

1.7 The *College of Wizardry* LARP at Czocha Castle, Poland 18

1.8 Potions class in the Castle Dungeon during the *College of Wizardry* LARP 19

1.9 Students eating in the Great Hall during the *College of Wizardry* LARP 20

2.1 Ten Reasons to play Breakout EDU 24

3.1 Librarians listen intently for the next clue in the *CSI: Library Murder Mystery* at the 2017 Michigan Library Association Conference 35

3.2 Librarians work in teams to piece together the parts of the puzzle 36

3.3 A library stamp is mulled over as the possible key to the mystery 36

5.1 Flowchart of *Alexander Hamilton Escape Room Game* 75

5.2 *Armada*, by Penny Page 78

5.3 Final lockbox with Chinese good luck cat statues 82

6.1 Organizers of the Michigan Library Association Breakout Game: Kathleen Zaenger, Janice Heilman, Brandi Tambasco, and Scott Drapalik of the Howell Carnegie District Library 93

6.2 Letter from the Mastermind 94

6.3 My team and me holding up our victory signs after we "broke out" 102

7.1 Chinese good luck cat statues 3-D printed and painted for my escape room 107

10.1 Google Form lock form for a digital escape game 127

10.2 Dracula jigsaw puzzle created at Jigsaw Planet 128

14.1 *Alexander Hamilton Escape Room* set-up 156

14.2 Investigator's table 157

14.3 Addison Adley's library carrel 158

14.4 Librarians solving the mystery 159

Preface

ESCAPE ROOMS AND IMMERSIVE EXPERIENCES HAVE BECOME AN outrageously popular pastime for people of all ages, intriguing young adults and seniors alike. They have been featured in television shows such as *The Real Housewives of Beverly Hills* and *Race to Escape* as well as films like *Escape Room* (2017). They have been adopted by libraries worldwide and have exploded from 2,800 rooms throughout the world in 2015 to over 7,200 in 2018.[1]

These immersive, interactive games that challenge players to solve a series of mental or physical puzzles within a time limit are a fantastic way to engage patrons with the library and pass along information literacy skills. This book will introduce you to the exciting world of escape rooms and immersive experiences and provide you with hands-on, practical instructions for how you can plan, design, and host these events yourself. You'll learn all about how you can design your own escape room games, run pop-up escape rooms, create clubs in which kids can create escape games, create digital and high-tech escape rooms, use these events for team-building and training, and more for your library!

As I saw libraries create escape room programs, I was thrilled. I am not only a librarian who is always on the lookout for new and exciting ways to involve patrons with library resources, but also a lifelong gamer. I got started with the greatest adventure game of all time, *The Legend of Zelda,* on my Nintendo system, and quickly moved to PC gaming in the early nineties. Armed with a boot disc, I played a slew of point-and-click and graphic adventure games that have served as major inspiration for today's escape room games such as *Maniac Mansion*, the *Quest for Glory*, *King's Quest*, the *Legend of Kyrandia* series, *Myst*, Roberta Williams's *Phantasmagoria*, the *Fable* series, *Syberia*, and one of my all-time favorites, *Zork Nemesis*. When I first encountered escape rooms and immersive experiences in 2015, I experienced a nostalgia that brought me back to those early gaming days that led me to start playing these games whenever I could. I even flew to Europe to participate in a four-day Harry Potter-inspired live action roleplaying (LARP) experience in a thirteenth-century Polish castle.

As the reader will discover, escape room games and immersive experiences programming have incredible potential for many library types including public, school, and academic libraries. These types of games and events are actively being used in libraries and education as a vehicle to provide valuable STEM, information literacy, and critical-thinking skills through game-based learning activities. They are a potent library advocacy and outreach tool that is being used by libraries at conferences and events as pop-up escape room or breakout experiences. Library staff and educators are also digitally designing them to support curriculum. Additionally, they are being customized for internal staff training as a more creative approach than traditional PowerPoint–based workshops as well as for team-building among sometimes widely dispersed library staff. In sum, these entertaining, interactive experiences have a vast array of imaginative applications for libraries, many of which will be discussed in this book along with detailed instructions for how you can implement them in your library today.

I would like to sincerely thank all the librarians and industry professionals who were interviewed, contributed projects and essays, and shared valuable professional advice.

NOTE

1. Starre Vartan, "Escape Rooms: Why People Flock to These 'Tourist Traps,'" *CNN Travel*, August 30, 2017, https://www.cnn.com/travel/article/escape-rooms-popular/index.html; Bo Moore, "Locked In: Behind the Scenes of the Escape Room Craze," *Make: Magazine*, https://makezine.com/2015/08/25/locked-in-behind-the-scenes-of-the-escape-room-craze/.

Introducing Escape Rooms and Immersive Experiences

1

Escape Rooms and Immersive Experiences Explained

ESCAPE ROOMS AND IMMERSIVE EVENTS ARE EXCITING NEW opportunities for libraries to engage patrons by making them a part of an experience. By combining elements of entertainment such as theater, video games, and movies, these new forms of leisure activities are capturing the attention of people throughout the world.

ESCAPE ROOMS

Escape rooms are live interactive adventure games in which participants must team up to solve a series of riddles, puzzles, and challenges to win. They have become immensely popular in recent years and have been featured on many television shows, including the Science Channel's *Race to Escape* series. According to CNN, "They're the No. 1 local activity for a number of cities around the world," and there are currently over 7,200 rooms in 1,445 cities in 105 countries. These games are set in a variety of fictional locations with themes as diverse as escaping the clutches of a zombie; breaking out of prison; or, in the all-ages *Kingdom of Cats*, avoiding capture by a society of felines. This new and wildly popular activity is already being embraced by libraries as a way to immerse patrons in critical-thinking exercises and much more. According to *American Libraries* magazine, escape rooms have become a breakout trend in youth programming.[1]

Inspired by adventure-style video games, these unique activities integrate audience participation, immersive theater, and gaming as tools to pass along problem-solving and collaboration skills, as well as old-fashioned entertainment to eager participants. And they are continuing to grow, nearly tripling in number since July 2015, when there were a mere 2,800 escape rooms worldwide. There have been several major library events that have incorporated this type of programming, for example, the New York Public Library's 2011 *Find the Future: The Game* event, an overnight scavenger hunt for which more than 5,000 people applied to participate. In 2014, the State Library of Western Australia hosted a sci-fi-themed escape room called *Memori* as a part of its 125th anniversary. And in 2015, the National Library of Singapore hosted *Escape from Reverie,* an escape room event that attracted over 1,000 participants during the single day it was open.[2]

This new and intriguing form of entertainment (and education) is continuing to evolve and develop as time goes on. Already we are seeing escape rooms designed for varying levels of participant experience, rooms designed for a specific number of players, games utilizing advanced technology such as Microsoft Kinect and Arduino boards to incorporate special effects, and rooms designed for repeated play with different puzzles for returning participants. And the growth of the industry has not yet shown signs of slowing down. According to the *Room Escape Artist*'s statistics, there were twenty-two escape room companies in the United States in 2014; at the end of the second quarter of 2017, there were more than 1,800.[3]

ORIGINS

Escape games have their roots in entertainment genres ranging from interactive theatre to haunted houses to video games. They utilize game theory and elements from the early interactive fiction computer games of the 1980s such as *Zork*, in which players must find items and solve puzzles through text-based interaction with the computer, as well as the graphic adventure games of the 1980s and early 1990s such as *King's Quest,* which relied on the player controlling their character with the mouse through a point-and-click interface. Finally, puzzle adventure games such as *Myst* and *Riven,* and escape-the-room online games such as *Crimson Room* and *MOTAS,* can all be said to have significantly influenced the development of today's escape room games.[4]

Live action roleplaying (LARP) games in which participants dress up as fictional characters and adopt personalities and mannerisms in an improvisational style for the span of a scenario or event became popular in the 1970s as an extension of *Dungeons and Dragons*–related tabletop gaming. The immersive nature of these games is also said to have inspired the creation of escape room games.[5]

Other precursors of today's escape games include scavenger hunts, including live-action and paper challenges such as those found in MIT's *Puzzle Hunt* (which began in 1981); interactive or immersive theatre experiences such as *Sleep No More,* an adaptation of Shakespeare's Macbeth in which the audience walks through several rooms of the performance at their own pace; interactive haunted houses such as Philadelphia's *Terror Behind the Walls,* which is set in the haunted Eastern State Penitentiary prison; and adventure reality television shows like *Survivor.*[6]

The first escape room, the Real Escape Game, was opened in Japan in 2007 as a single room. It was designed by Takao Kato of the SCRAP publishing company. In 2011, Hungary's Parapark facility opened in Budapest. Escape room games became extremely popular throughout Asia and parts of Europe. In 2012 they debuted in the United States when the Real Escape Game opened in San Francisco.[7]

TYPES OF ESCAPE ROOMS

Escape room games are interactive games in which groups of participants gather in a room where they must solve a series of puzzles within a specified time limit (most often one hour) to win, or "escape the room." They are immersive live action games that give players the experience of being the central characters in a movie or a video game. They can take place in settings ranging from a crime scene to a wizard's tower. They can employ all manner of props and theatrical devices to add atmosphere and tension to scenarios about impending pandemics, chemical plants on the verge of meltdown, or rescues of damsels in distress. Escape rooms are imaginative, perplexing, and thoroughly captivating forms of entertainment for people of all ages and backgrounds.[8]

FIGURE 1.1
Escape Thrill's *Wild West Room*

At Escape Thrill, you find yourself in a room with yellowed wallpaper, aging wooden furniture, and a wagon-wheel chandelier. You realize that you're in a Wild West saloon and to solve the room you must discover who shot Wild Bill Hickock by using clues such as the final hand dealt at the poker table (see figure 1.1).

FIGURE 1.2
My mother and me with our gamemaster at Escape Countdown Tampa before our *Jailbreak* game

This is only one scenario. In other rooms such as *Vault 13* in Berlin's Claustrophobia escape rooms, you may find that you and your group are the sole survivors of a nuclear war who must work together to escape an underground shelter. Romania's Codex escape game features one that takes place in a speakeasy circa the Roaring Twenties in which players must infiltrate Al Capone's gang. The Escape Game Chicago launches players into space with their *Mission Mars* room, in which participants must repair their ship and escape the red planet before succumbing to cosmic radiation.

Escape games employ all manner of themes and tropes to entertain their visitors. Some use costumes and uniforms not only for their staff, but for players as well. At Escape Countdown in Tampa, Florida, players must don orange correctional-facility jumpsuits and handcuffs (figure 1.2) before entering the *Jailbreak* game room, which starts off with the players inside a small jail cell.

LEVELS OF DIFFICULTY

Escape rooms also have varying levels of difficulty designed for players at the beginner, advanced, and expert levels. It is important to determine the degree of difficulty before booking because novice players will end up frustrated if they unwittingly take on an expert room. Unfortunately, many escape game websites do not provide this information in their room descriptions. However, a quick call to the escape room will usually yield this information.

The number of players per room is also significant. Rooms have a minimum (usually two) and a maximum number of players that will be allowed in the room. Small parties may be placed in with another group who booked for the same time. It is important to note the number of players for which the room was designed, because this will also give some indication of level of difficulty. For example, if a room's capacity is two to eight players, you can estimate that there will usually be four to six players taking on the room's challenges at the same time. So, while the escape room will usually let a party of just two reserve the room, you can be sure that both people will have to work double-time to get through all the puzzles in the allotted time period. Some rooms such as *An Evening in Paris* at Escape Countdown Tampa (figure 1.3) have been specifically designed for "date night," and created for only two players.

FIGURE 1.3
An Evening in Paris escape game designed for two at Escape Countdown Tampa

When choosing an escape room another factor to consider is success rate. This is the rate at which the room has been solved. This information is sometimes provided on the escape room's website, but many times is not. A phone call to the establishment will provide this information because updated statistics are kept on player wins, and so on. This is important to know if you have people in your group who are new to this style of game. They are more apt to enjoy themselves in a room with a high escape rate rather than starting off with a room with a 19 percent escape rate.

PLAYERS

Part of the appeal of escape room games is that everyone is on equal footing. All the information required to solve the puzzles and find the necessary clues can be found within the room. Prior knowledge is not required, which makes

FIGURE 1.4
Three generations of my family about to play the *Legends of Atlantis* escape room at Backstage Escape Games, Myrtle Beach, South Carolina

them great entertainment for diverse groups or families (figure 1.4). These live, participatory puzzle-style games are enjoyed by people of all ages from children to adults (both women and men). According to a survey of 175 escape room facilities worldwide, groups that visit escape games are made up of people of all ages. Groups of adults over twenty-one make up 37 percent of player groups and young adults under twenty-one make up 19 percent. The gender ratio is 14 percent all-female groups to 15 percent all-male groups, with mixed gender groups comprising 71 percent.[9]

Corporate clients such as Microsoft, Netflix, and Amazon make up a large portion of the revenue stream for escape room games. These are excellent team-building events that many corporations use not only to encourage staff unity but to identify leaders who take charge and demonstrate quick thinking during these games. At Escape Expert Dallas, part of the corporate package includes an optional competition between players in different rooms as well as video footage of teams playing and solving the room for clients to review afterwards.[10]

THE ESCAPE ROOM EXPERIENCE

When players arrive at an escape room facility they are usually greeted by the gamemaster who will administer their game. Participants are asked to sign an accident waiver and release of liability form before playing the game, which sets the tone from the start that this will be both a physical and interactive experience. The gamemaster then explains the rules for that particular room; for example, whether dismantling certain objects in the room such as thermostats, light fixtures, and so on, is allowed or not (I have experienced both types). There is usually mention that outside tools are not allowed within the room as there have been cases of over-eager players dismantling escape room settings with their own tools that they brought along. The time limit is given, and players are referred to where they can check their time and how they can receive hints during gameplay. Escape games are most often monitored by the gamemaster via closed circuit television and he/she is usually standing by to watch for any problems players may be having.

Some escape rooms provide technology like tablets or touch screens from which players can receive hints and/or keep track of their progress, while others provide chalkboards or whiteboards for players to keep notes on. Most escape rooms will have some sort of monitor in the room through which the gamemaster can provide clues to players who most often request clues verbally when they are stuck. All of this information will be explained to players before they begin their quest to escape the room.

To start the game, the gamemaster will read players the background scenario to set the stage and perhaps play an introductory video. Players are then left to their own devices and the countdown clock begins. Everything in the room, save the few out-of-bounds areas mentioned by the gamemaster, is investigated by participants. Letters of correspondence, paintings on the walls, calendars, journals, maps, and even furniture is pored over and carefully inspected by players as they decipher secret codes, unlock puzzles, and find hidden objects that lead them to the final key that will open the door and solve the game.

ESCAPE GAMES THROUGHOUT THE WORLD

Escape room games can vary greatly in theme and setting; however, in the United States most take one hour to complete and run about $30 per person to play. Most have online booking systems. Most set minimum age at which children can participate from twelve to fourteen years.

Escape Rooms in the United States

Komnata Quest in New York City (https://komnataquest.com) was named the best escape room in the United States, topping the *USA Today's* 2017 List of the Best Escape Rooms. It has eighteen rooms with various games designed for two people, for children, and for adults only. For gamers, there is a *Fallout*-themed room called *The Vault*, games for comic book fans like *The Joker's Cafe*, and others in the genres of steampunk, horror, adventure, and mystery, including the *Sherlocked* room.[11]

Coming in at second on *USA Today's* 2017 list, Enchambered Live Escape Room Adventure in Sacramento, California (https://www.enchambered.com), has four rooms including *Containment Breach*, which takes place in a mad scientist's lab; a gothic ghost room called *The Whispering Halls*, which takes place in a Victorian manor; a horror room set in a swamp called *The Skull Witch*, and *The Hidden Tomb*, an Indiana Jones–inspired adventure room.[12]

Voted the third-best escape game in the nation in 2017, Cross Roads Escape Games in Anaheim, California (https://crossroadsescapegames.com), has two games. *The Hex Room* challenges players to survive a horror movie in which they play roles cast ahead of time; they are divided into separate rooms where they must work individually and in groups to survive. *The Fun House* is a circus-themed, family-friendly game that welcomes children by asking them if they are a clown or a magician.[13]

Fourth on the *USA Today* 2017 list is 5 Wits (http://5-wits.com), located in Massachusetts, Pennsylvania, and New York. It has five escape games across their locations, including *Espionage*, a Mission Impossible–inspired game complete with laser motion-sensor lights and *Drago's Castle*, a medieval quest that challenges players to escape a dungeon and capture a dragon. *20,000 Leagues* takes players on an undersea adventure aboard Captain Nemo's ship Nautilus, *Tomb* transports participants to an Egyptian archaeological dig where they must escape the spirit of an ancient Pharaoh, and finally *Deep Space* treats players to a space battle aboard an abandoned starship.[14]

Escape Code (https://www.escapecode.tv/) located in Branson, Missouri, ranked fifth on the 2017 *USA Today* list. It features five escape games, two of which are Bible adventures: *The Arrival*, which takes place in a stable in Bethlehem, and *Condemned*, which follows Paul and Silas into a Roman prison. Other games include *Vortex*, in which players must escape a catastrophic storm, and two horror-themed rooms; *The Guest House* and *Revenge*.[15]

60OUT Escape Rooms (http://www.60out.com) boasts twenty rooms across their various locations in Los Angeles and Philadelphia. Its main location is in Los Angeles, so it is not surprising that most of these rooms are film-inspired quests, including their *Jumanji* and *Titanic* rooms. Other escape rooms include *Dracula*, *Da Vinci's Secret*, *Hangover*, *The Krampus*, and *Alice in Wonderland*. It was voted tenth-best escape room on the 2017 *USA Today* list.[16]

Other escape rooms on the 2017 *USA Today* list include 60 to Escape in Gurnee, Illinois; Breakout Lawrence in Lawrence, Kansas; Escape Room Insomnia DC in Washington, DC and Virginia; and Omescape, headquartered in San Jose, California.[17]

The Tampa Bay Escape Room (www.tampabayescaperoom.com/) was Tampa Bay, Florida's first live escape room experience. It boasts four rooms including *Tragic Magic* (figure 1.5), a fantastical game set in a wizard's keep; *Kidnapped,* which transports players into a hostage situation; and the horror-themed *Cabin in the Woods*.

FIGURE 1.5
The *Tragic Magic* game room at the Tampa Bay Escape Room

The Escape Game (https://theescapegamechicago.com/) has locations in Chicago, as well as Texas, Minnesota, Tennessee, and Florida, is well-known for its immersive games including *Prison Break, Gold Rush, Special Ops, Mission Mars,* and *The Heist*.

New Orleans' first escape room is Clue Carré (https://www.cluecarre.com), which entices its visitors with *The Voodoo Room,* in which players must follow clues hidden by voodoo queen Marie Laveau; the *Haunted Swamp Room,* which tasks participants to vanquish a ghost; the *Vampire Hunter,* in which players must locate a hidden stake and defeat Antoine Devillier, New Orleans' most bloodthirsty vampire; and the *French Quarter House of Curiosities*, which traps its visitors for eternity.

Breakout KC (https://breakoutkc.com) was ranked in the top five escape games by both *USA Today* (in 2016) and Trip Advisor. It is located in Kansas City, Missouri, and Leawood, Kansas. All of its rooms are family-friendly and open to all ages. Their games include *Under Cover,* an FBI mission; a prison break in the time of the Civil War; a game that challenges players to save the world from the Y2K bug; *The Gambler,* set in a casino; and Room 13, set in an eerie hotel room that holds players captive.

Escape Thrill of Clearwater, Florida, has five enthralling rooms, including *Deadline,* which puts players in the midst of a high-tech secret intelligence agency interview where they must work under pressure to solve problems using virtual reality equipment. Other rooms include *Skinned Alive,* in which players must escape the basement of a serial killer; *The Toy Room,* a kid-friendly room in which a world of toys comes to life; *Wild West,* which challenges players to capture the killer of Wild Bill Hickok; and *Diamond Heist,* which tasks players to steal a priceless gem.

Real Escape Game (https://realescapegame.com) with locations in San Francisco, San Jose, Los Angeles, and Toronto, Ontario, is created and owned by SCRAP, inventors of the first known escape game, which opened in 2007 in Japan. This is the company that started it all. It was ranked number one on the Best Escape Room List in *USA Today* list in 2016. It has eleven escape room games across its locations including *Escape from the Time Travel Lab, The Mummy, Spellbound Supper,* and *Pacific Rim.*[18]

Escape Countdown (https://www.escapecountdown.com) has multiple locations throughout Florida and features captivating rooms such as *The Boiler Room,* in which players must escape the clutches of a serial killer; the more romantic *An Evening in Paris* room (see figure 1.3), designed just for two; as well as other adventures such as the *Jail Break* room, the *Mad Hatter* game, and the pirate-themed *Escape from Gaspar Island.*

International Escape Rooms

There are thousands of escape rooms worldwide. Here is a selection of the more well-known international escape room experiences. Note that many international escape games are priced based on size of party versus the individual pricing of rooms in the United States.

Great Britain

Escape Reality (https://www.escapereality.com) has rooms in Edinburgh and Glasgow, Scotland, as well as throughout the United Kingdom, United States, and Dubai. It features the *Tortuga Pirates* room, the horror-themed *Asylum* and *Nosferatu* rooms, the sci-fi *Machina* game, and the *Escape from Alcatraz* room.

ClueQuest (https://cluequest.co.uk) is a live escape game in London that was voted the #1 such attraction in the city on TripAdvisor. Games include *Plan52* for beginners, *Operation BlackSheep* for more experienced players, and *Professor BlackSheep* for escape room experts.

France

Rated the best escape game in Paris (https://www.thegame-france.com), The Game features seven escape game experiences including a *Casino Heist*, a *Kidnapping*, an adventure in the *Catacombs* beneath the city, and a search for the *Treasure of the Templars*.

Germany

Claustrophobia (https://berlin.claustrophobia.com/en), located in Berlin, Germany, features a trio of adventure-filled escape games including *The Vault*, a post-apocalyptic/*Fallout*-inspired escape room; *Pirate's Hut*, which pits players against a bloodthirsty pirate; and *Museum of Contemporary Art*, in which players take part in a museum heist.

The Netherlands

Escape Room Nederland (https://escaperoom.nl) is the top escape room in Holland. It features three surrealistic rooms, *The Laboratory of Dr. Steiner*, *The Girl's Room*, and the sci-fi themed *The Dome*. Players can watch highlights of their game in the lounge afterwards.

Hungary

E-Exit (Emergency Exit) Games (http://szabadulos-jatek.hu/en.) is ranked the top escape room in Budapest, Hungary. It features four rooms with varying levels of difficulty, including the advanced *Santa Muerte* game, in which players must find the Sombrero of Life to survive Saint Death; the intermediate *Heaven and Hell* room and *1984* room (based on George Orwell's novel); and the easy *Circus* room, in which players must set all the animals free. Also in Budapest, Claustrophilia (http://claustrophilia.hu/en/index.html) features just one room—*The Wicklewood Heritage*, which takes place in the apartment of Lord Wicklewood, an eminent adventurer who left behind clues to the world's most sought-after treasures.

Romania

The Codex (www.thecodex.ro/en) in Bucharest, Romania, features both escape games and challenge rooms that are part escape room, part strategic board game; players are pitted against another team to beat the 90-minute clock and solve all puzzles. It also has an escape room designed for children called *The Detectives*, which specifies a maximum age of sixteen to play. Other rooms include the *Prohibition* room, which transports players into Al Capone's speakeasy; *Secret Society,* a medieval game in which players must pass a secret cult's initiation ceremony; and *Sleepy Hollow,* a game in which participants must work together to remove an evil curse.

Immersive Experiences

In 2013, the Museum of Modern Art in New York City invited visitors to step inside a rainstorm that would not get them wet and that they could control with the movement of their bodies. This incredibly popular and interactive *Rain Room* drew 1,000 people a day, many of whom waited hours in line, to MoMA, and another 190,000 visitors during its fifteen-month stint in Los Angeles when it was loaned to LACMA. This is just one type of immersive experience that is changing people's expectations of how they interact with art, pop-culture, and exhibits.[19]

Fans of the hit television show *CSI* can visit *CSI: The Experience* in Las Vegas, where instead of just viewing sets and props used in the series, players are given an interactive experience. Visitors don official CSI vests and become crime scene investigators, gathering evidence at the scene, conducting forensic analysis, and then cracking the case.

Today's immersive experiences transform the visitor from a passive onlooker to a fully engrossed participant, and they are proving that people will wait all day in line to become part of a narrative rather than just listen to a story. These types of immersive experiences and exhibits put visitors in the driver's seat and offer them the active role they desire. Some add elements of gamification to engross their visitors, while other exhibits make the visitor a part of the installation itself. Either way, these experiential exhibits and events are where people are choosing to spend their time and money.

Interactive Museum Exhibits

Interactive and immersive museum exhibits attract throngs of visitors eager to become a part of a work of art or to learn through experiencing an exhibit. These types of exhibits draw not only museum goers but also those who might not typically visit a museum but have seen images of the attractions on social media sites such as Instagram and Facebook.

A new exhibit at the Smithsonian's Sackler Gallery takes visitors on a journey to a living Buddhist site in Sri Lanka via a meditative digital film projected onto three large screens that show the daily practices of monks and nuns during the December full-moon festival. *Encountering the Buddha: Art and Practice across Asia* also invites visitors to enter a lamplit Tibetan Buddhist shrine room filled with 243 objects created by Tibetan, Chinese, Nepalese, and Mongolian artists of the thirteenth to nineteenth centuries. None of the objects are encased in glass but are arranged as they would be in the shrine room of a noble family. This is just one example of how museums are changing the experience for their visitors. Instead of providing sterile glass cases filled with hundreds of objects for visitors to walk by, they created an experience by offering them the chance to immerse themselves in a sacred space.[20]

The American Museum of Natural History has opened a new experiential exhibition filled with eleven funhouse-like interactive galleries that explore sight, smell, sound, touch, taste, and balance. *Our Senses: An Immersive Experience* investigates how the human brain works with the sensory organs to shape perceptions of the world. A black-and-white room challenges visitors' sense of balance with a flat floor juxtaposed against rippling walls, a space with changing lights will challenge sight and perception by revealing different images, and a smell test will invite visitors to make sense of a particular odor. Visitors are also treated to a bee's-eye view of a giant garden and challenged to track specific sounds in an audio collage.[21]

In 2017 The teamLab: *Transcending Boundaries* exhibit in the Pace Gallery London engulfed visitors in a spectacular, interactive light and sound exhibit made up of multiple installations. The *Universe of Water Particles* featured an interactive waterfall of light that flowed throughout the gallery that allowed visitors to walk over and within the streams of water, which reacted to their movements. They could interact with the nearby work, *The Flutter of Butterflies Beyond Borders, Ephemeral Life*, which spawned digital butterflies where they stood. The breathtaking *Flowers Bloom on People* installation presented a dark room that bloomed flowers on visitors as they stood and spread to others to connect them. The entire lifecycle of the flowers was represented from buds to blossoms to eventual decay.[22]

Museums have also begun using augmented reality (AR) technology to add interactive elements and bring artwork and exhibits to life. AR tools allow people to view layers of information projected over the real world through their mobile devices. Both the Royal Ontario Museum and the Smithsonian Museum have used these applications to bring dinosaurs to life, adding flesh and movement to displayed bones as visitors view them through their smartphones. Using an AR app, visitors to the National Museum of Singapore's *Story of the Forest* exhibit can hunt for and collect animals and plants within a 558-foot-long animated digital mural of sixty-nine drawings of flora and fauna created by Japanese art collective teamLab. The British Museum uses AR for museum education, challenging kids to learn about Greece in the fifth century BCE as they play an augmented reality game while exploring the Parthenon Gallery. The Cleveland Museum of Art is using AR technology in conjunction with the Microsoft Kinect by tracking their movements and adding augmented reality effects which respond to them. For example, visitors can mold clay in the 3-D space as well as throw virtual paint onto a digital canvas to create a Jackson Pollock–inspired painting.[23]

At my workplace, the New York Law Institute, we used AR technology to create an augmented reality rare books exhibit (see figure 1.6) in which we showcased many of our rare holdings such as *The Law Register of Alexander Hamilton*, General George Washington's copy of *Corbin's Le Code Louis XIII*, and John Jay's copy of *The Present Practice of the High Court of Chancery*. The *Treasures and Technology of the New York Law Institute* exhibit invited patrons to glimpse inside our rare treasures without damaging the books themselves. By waving their devices in front of each book, patrons were given video, image, and text overlays that provided information about what was inside. We printed out photos of each librarian and put them on display in the exhibit. As patrons viewed librarians' still photos, videos were cleverly overlaid to make them appear to come to life like portraits in a Harry Potter book or film. And our patrons were amazed. They couldn't wait to get to the next item to discover what types of videos and information would be hidden inside.

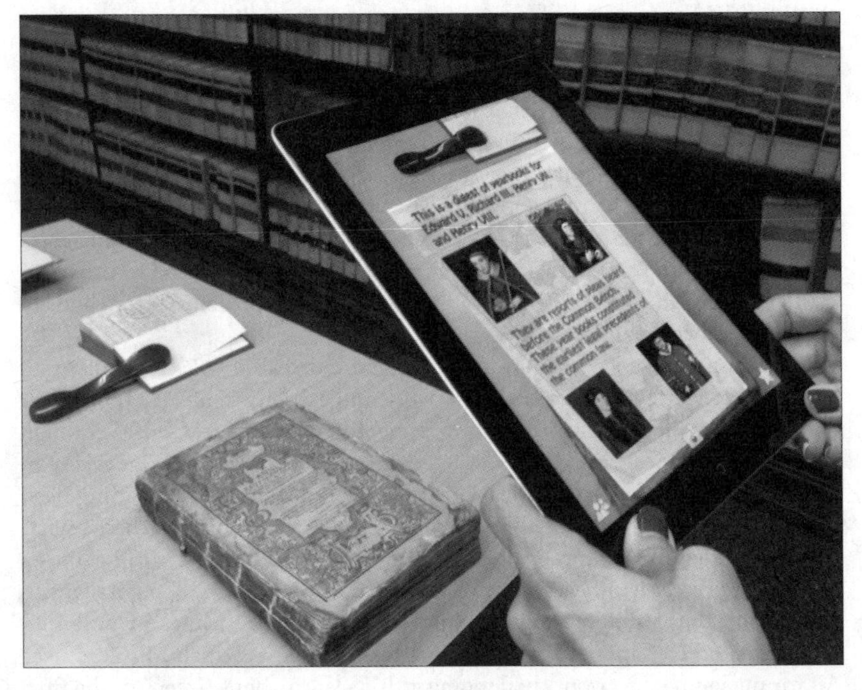

FIGURE 1.6
An augmented reality rare books exhibit titled the *Treasures and Technology of the New York Law Institute* immersed visitors in the library's collections

Immersive Fandom and Cinematic Experiences

Like interactive museum exhibits, immersive movie-based exhibitions and events have become popular attractions. These types of exhibits are comparable to escape rooms in that many of them involve challenges and a gaming element, although they are typically activities for a single person whereas escape rooms are designed for groups. They are also more casual, missing the time constraints and the locked-in component. Many of them simply immerse the participant in the world of the film, television show, or a book.

The *Marvel Avengers S.T.A.T.I.O.N.* is an immersive and interactive exhibit that educates visitors about the world of the Avengers. Visitors train to become official agents of the S.T.A.T.I.O.N. as they explore the Marvel Cinematic Universe through props and costumes from the Avengers films. Visitors to *DreamWorks Tours Shrek's Adventure! London* board a magical 4-D tour bus to Far Far Away where they visit Shrek's swamp, meet Puss in Boots, rescue Pinocchio, and cast a spell with the Muffin Man. Visitors must find all the special ingredients to locate Shrek and return home.

Visitors to *The Wizarding World of Harry Potter* at Universal Studios in Orlando, Florida, can ride the Hogwarts Express, dine in the Leaky Cauldron, walk through Diagon Alley and pick out a wand at Ollivanders, and partake in the Harry Potter and the Escape from Gringotts multidimensional ride.[24]

AVATAR: Discover Pandora is a new interactive exhibition in Shenzhen, China, inspired by James Cameron's film *Avatar.* This 12,000-square-foot entertainment and educational experience opened in January 2018 invites visitors to the twenty-second-century world of Pandora. Visitors can interact with Avatar creatures, discover the wonders of space travel and the moon Pandora, learn about the Na'vi and how they live, and explore Pandora's breathtaking environments.[25]

Disney has announced a new fully immersive *Star Wars* resort to open in 2019. Guests will become citizens of the galaxy and will be given a story line that will touch every minute of their days. The hotel will be designed as if it were the interior of a space ship and all windows in the resort will show starry skies rather than the Florida sun.[26]

Libraries are already incorporating immersive fandom experiences into their programming with Harry Potter-themed Yule Balls, Dr. Who-themed library lock-ins and events, and more.

Live Action Roleplaying Games

In November 2015, I boarded a bus in Berlin, Germany, that took me to the countryside of Poland to take part in a Harry Potter-inspired live action role-playing game, or LARP (see figure 1.7). For the next four days I attended the College of Wizardry with 150 other "students" in a thirteenth-century castle. During the days we attended classes such as the speculative Magical Theory; Dark Arts Defense, which involved raising and then controlling demons;

FIGURE 1.7
The *College of Wizardry* LARP at Czocha Castle, Poland

Arithromancy, which discussed topics such as golem ethics; and the hands-on Potions class, in which students created healing elixirs and harming brews (see figure 1.8). Nights were spent skipping curfew and narrowly evading the teachers to seek out hidden passages.

Once, at midnight, we had a clandestine meeting in the dungeon to raise a spirit, on another we snuck into the Dark Forest and were chased by a werewolf, and on yet another we sipped honey beer in the nearby tavern. My classmates and I ate our meals together in the Knights Hall (see figure 1.9), sang our school anthem at the opening of the Student Ball, discovered the secret Mirror Room behind the teacher's lounge, accidentally raised a demon instead of a prefect, learned to Polka, and antagonized many a teacher. In short, we had the time of our lives!

The large-scale live action roleplaying game *College of Wizardry* (https://www.wizardry.college) is organized by Dziobak LARP Studios. It also hosts Fairweather Manor (https://www.fmlarp.com), a LARP inspired by Downton Abbey in which participants can take on the roles of the manor's family and servants, artists, and local guests. This Edwardian LARP takes place in Moszna Castle, Poland. *Convention of Thorns* (https://www.cotlarp.com) is a vampire-themed LARP filled with political intrigue and the decadence of

FIGURE 1.8
Potions class in the Castle Dungeon during the *College of Wizardry* LARP

FIGURE 1.9
Students eating in the Great Hall during the *College of Wizardry* LARP

vampire society. Players join a vampire clan in the late fifteenth century and, in the course of three nights in the Polish castle of Zamek Ksiaz, vie for power. *Demeter* (https://www.demeterlarp.com) is a gothic horror LARP about Dracula's voyage to England. This LARP takes place on an actual sailing ship that travels the Baltic Sea between Germany and Denmark. *Skull and Crossbones* (https://www.saclarp.com) is a pirate sailing adventure LARP that sails three ships on the Baltic Sea between Germany and Denmark. Participants take on the roles of buccaneers and learn how to sail a traditional sailing ship.

NOTES

1. Bo Moore, "Locked In: Behind the Scenes of the Escape Room Craze," *Make: Magazine*, https://makezine.com/2015/08/25/locked-in-behind-the-scenes-of-the-escape-room-craze/; Katie O'Reilly, "Libraries on Lockdown: Escape Rooms a Breakout Trend in Youth Programming," *American Libraries*,

September 1, 2016, https://americanlibrariesmagazine.org/2016/09/01/escape-rooms-libraries-on-lockdown/.

2. O'Reilly, "Libraries on Lockdown"; Derek Murphy, "Library Escape Rooms: Keeping Your Patrons Captive," *Unbound*, April 14, 2016, http://slis.simmons.edu/blogs/unbound/2016/04/14/library-escape-rooms/.
3. Lisa Spira, "Three Years of Room Escapes: The Growth of the US Market," *Room Escape Artist,* July 30, 2017, https://roomescapeartist.com/2017/07/30/three-years-of-room-escapes-the-growth-of-the-us-market/.
4. S. Nicholson, "Peeking behind the Locked Door: A Survey of Escape Room Facilities," white paper, http://scottnicholson.com/pubs/erfacwhite.pdf.
5. Ibid.
6. Ibid.
7. Ibid.
8. Claire Reilly, "Inside the Enigma: The Tech behind an Escape Room," *CNet,* March 12, 2015, https://www.cnet.com/news/inside-the-enigma-room-the-technology-behind-an-escape-room/.
9. Nicholson, "Peeking behind the Locked Door."
10. Sally French and Jessica Marmor Shaw, "The Unbelievably Lucrative Business of Escape Rooms," *MarketWatch,* July 21, 2015, https://www.marketwatch.com/story/the-weird-new-world-of-escape-room-businesses-2015-07-20; Corporate Team Building. Escape Expert. https://www.escapeexpert.com/corporate.
11. "10 Best Escape Rooms Reader's Choice Awards 2017," *USA Today,* www.10best.com/awards/travel/best-escape-room-2017/.
12. Ibid.
13. Ibid.
14. Ibid.
15. Ibid.
16. Ibid.
17. Ibid.
18. "10 Best Escape Rooms: Reader's Choice Awards 2016," *USA Today,* www.10best.com/awards/travel/best-escape-room-2016/.
19. David Ng, "'Rain Room' Installation Simulating Downpour Coming to LACMA," *Los Angeles Times,* July 7, 2015, www.latimes.com/entertainment/arts/culture/la-et-cm-rain-room-lacma-20150706-story.html; Michael Juliano, "'Rain Room' Is Staying with LACMA for Good," *Time Out Los Angeles,* January 31, 2017. https://www.timeout.com/los-angeles/blog/rain-room-is-staying-with-lacma-for-good-013117.
20. "Smithsonian's Sackler Gallery Explores Rich Buddhist Heritage of Asia: 'Encountering the Buddha: Art and Practice across Asia,'" *Smithsonian Newsdesk,* July 27, 2017, https://newsdesk.si.edu/releases/smithsonian-s-sackler-gallery-explores-rich-buddhist-heritage-asia.

21. "The American Museum of Natural History Announces the New Exhibition Our Senses: An Immersive Experience," American Museum of Natural History, https://www.amnh.org/about-the-museum/press-center/our-senses-an-immersive-experience.
22. "teamLab: Transcending Boundaries," Pace Gallery, https://www.pacegallery.com/exhibitions/12840/transcending-boundaries.
23. Jennifer Billock, "Five Augmented Reality Experiences That Bring Museum Exhibits to Life," Smithsonian.com, June 29, 2017, https://www.smithsonianmag.com/travel/expanding-exhibits-augmented-reality-180963810/; Natasha Baker, "Dinosaurs Roar to Life with Museum's Augmented Reality App," *The Globe and Mail,* July 16, 2012, updated March 26, 2017, https://www.theglobeandmail.com/technology/tech-news/dinosaurs-roar-to-life-with-museums-augmented-reality-app/article4420174/; Tom Anstey, "National Museum of Singapore Unveils 170 m-Long Digital Interactive Forest Installation," *Attractions Management,* December 21, 2016, www.attractionsmanagement.com/detail.cfm?pagetype=detail&subject=news&codeID=329222; "School Digital Session, Self-Led Session: A Gift for Athena," The British Museum, www.britishmuseum.org/learning/schools_and_teachers/sessions/a_gift_for_athena.aspx; Jennifer Kite-Powell, "Augmented Reality and Kinect Create Unique Art Experience at Cleveland Museum," *Forbes Tech,* October 27, 2016, https://www.forbes.com/sites/jenniferhicks/2016/10/27/augmented-reality-and-kincect-create-unique-art-experience-at-cleveland-museum/#5509982b3771.
24. Christina Green, "6 Immersive Exhibitions that Became Attractions," *Event Manager Blog,* February 17, 2017, www.eventmanagerblog.com/immersive-exhibitions-attractions.
25. Avatar: Discover Pandora, www.avatardiscoverpandora.com.
26. Carlye Wisel, "You Can Soon Stay in a Fully Immersive Star Wars Hotel," *Travel and Leisure,* July 17, 2017, www.travelandleisure.com/trip-ideas/disney-vacations/disney-star-wars-hotel.

2

The Escape Room Opportunity

ESCAPE ROOMS AND IMMERSIVE EXPERIENCES CAN BE USED BY libraries in a number of ways: to teach information literacy skills in an engaging way, to add unique youth programming, to bring adults into the library, to teach patrons about library resources by using puzzles and challenges, and, because these experiences can easily be made portable, for outreach. Many people enjoy being at the center of the action rather than being a passive observer, and experiential learning theory has shown that hands-on learning has a great impact on learners. Escape rooms and immersive experiences can be an enticing and educational tool for this type of instruction. They are already being used as such; Breakout EDU is an immersive learning games platform that has developed escape room kits for instructors to facilitate, specializing in K-12 experiences. As indicated by figure 2.1, there are many opportunities for libraries to provide positive educational and skill-building outcomes with escape room games.

STEM LEARNING THROUGH ESCAPE ROOMS

Libraries are in a unique position to offer STEM (science, technology, engineering, and math) learning opportunities to patrons outside of the classroom in a fun and engaging way, without the pressure of grades. Teaching STEM skills through escape room games is one such opportunity. Escape room games, especially those designed with specific learning outcomes, like

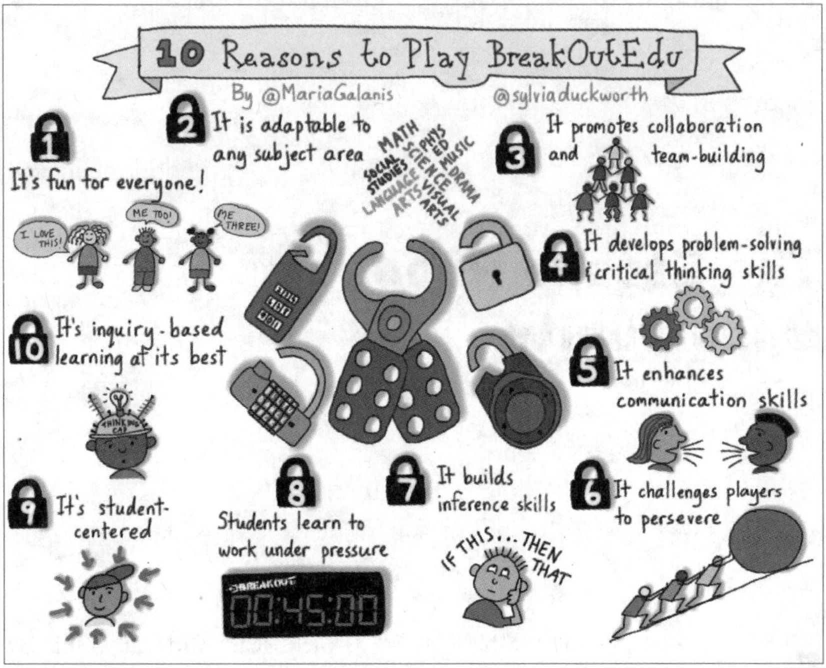

Artwork by Sylvia Duckworth: http://sylviaduckworth.com

FIGURE 2.1
Ten reasons to play Breakout EDU

those found on the Breakout EDU website (www.BreakoutEDU.com) can teach kids about subjects such as math, science, and computers while engrossing them in gameplay. Kids can learn math skills by trying to unlock an alien fuel pod or discover an ancient Babylonian treasure. Through escape games, they can learn the basics of chemistry by attending a potions class in a wizarding school or learn the fundamentals of DNA by saving the human race from harmful radiation. They can learn computer programming by time-traveling to the Jurassic Era or locating a lost pirate treasure. They can do all of this via library programming and events.[1]

Game-based learning has become a well-established method of teaching, and escape room games fit well into this niche. There are hundreds of math, science, and computer-related escape games available at no cost online, and the possibilities are endless when it comes to developing new escape games that support STEM learning. These games challenge players while at the same time exciting them about STEM topics to which they might not otherwise be exposed. Frank Lantz, director of the Game Center at New York University, put it well when he said, "All games, by their very nature, have a deep relationship to the core STEM skills of logic and reason, empiricism, the scientific method."[2]

INFORMATION LITERACY INSTRUCTION

It's always challenging to come up with creative and engaging ways to teach information literacy skills to library patrons. What better way to go about it than by gamifying the experience through an escape room challenge? A library's group study room or computer lab can be transformed into a top-secret government facility or nuclear power plant that must be shut down by finding hidden passcodes and clues among the library's resources. Librarians can design the room from scratch or else easily tailor an existing escape room game to meet the needs of their instructional sessions. The projects in chapters 4 and 5 provide instructions on how to implement both options.

LIBRARY ORIENTATION TOURS

Incoming students or new library patrons can be taken on a tour of the library via an escape room experience. Lock combinations and secret passwords can by hidden within different areas of the library in a scavenger-hunt style. Libraries can organize these types of rooms around breakout boxes that can be unlocked by the teamwork of groups of students or library patrons who follow clues that orient them to the library while locating the missing pieces of the puzzles, like the third project, How to Create a Pop-Up Escape Room, discussed in chapter 6.

STAFF TRAINING AND TEAM-BUILDING

In addition to providing learning opportunities for patrons, escape room games are fantastic vehicles for building teamwork and cooperation. They can be used to encourage staff to build connections and get to know their coworkers in a fun and entertaining environment. They can also be tailored to transform dry staff training programs into intriguing experiences that will be eagerly anticipated by library staff. Learning through play and building relationships with fellow coworkers will have a much more positive outcome than a mandatory workshop session given as a lecture. The project in chapter 12 discusses how to host an escape room event for team-building and training.

CURRICULUM SUPPORT

Escape rooms can be designed explicitly for a particular class or to support a larger curriculum within a school library or academic environment. They present great opportunities for librarians to partner with faculty in the learning process while providing an innovative program that encourages analytical thinking. As discussed throughout the project chapters in part 2, escape games can be easily tailored to fit any set of learning outcomes by adjusting the puzzle types and narrative.

CRITICAL THINKING AND OTHER SKILLS

The types of challenges found in most escape room games encourage the development of problem-solving and critical-thinking skills. Although puzzles can sometimes be based on previous knowledge or trivia, the majority of puzzle types discussed in chapter 5 necessitate the use of logic and reason to come up with the correct solution. Because these are games, the fear of failure that students might have about coming up with the wrong answer within the classroom is removed. In an escape room, players dive right in, try out a solution; if it doesn't work, they can quickly adjust their strategies and try different tactics. Other important life skills such as socialization and teamwork can also be passed along through the cooperative play of escape rooms.

Major Rex Thomen, a professor of Military Science for the Army Reserve Officers' Training Corps (ROTC), has successfully used escape room games to teach his military students valuable critical-thinking skills in a setting that frees them from instructor bias.[3]

> The biggest surprise in conducting the escape room was the emergence of different leaders. These were the students who usually didn't take charge due to a lack of confidence in their military knowledge. However, when playing the escape game they were a force, finding solutions from giant leaps in logic. Now I am constantly engaging them on what they see and what courses of action they see as viable. Definitely found some leaders who can think outside the box.[4]

LIBRARY ADVOCACY

Escape room games are a fantastic tool for library advocacy, as discussed in this excellent contribution by Nicole Scherer, Outreach Services Specialist at the Nassau (NY) Library System, (Former Head of Teen Services, Fairfield (Connecticut) Public Library).

Getting Frothy
On Escape Rooms and Library Advocacy

I enjoy telling strangers that I'm a librarian. It's great when people reply that they love libraries, or reading, or whatever, but I really get a kick out of the other response. You know the ones I'm talking about: "Really? That's still a thing?" or "Does anyone even use libraries anymore?" or, "Wow, I haven't been to a library in forever." I love it because, more often than not, it leads to conversations that invariably end the same way—with the other person exclaiming something along the lines of "I didn't know libraries did that!"

That "I didn't know . . ." is frustrating to many of us, for good reason—it means that despite our efforts, users aren't aware of all the things we have done to reshape ourselves to be of better service to our evolving communities. It means that too many people maintain an outdated view of who we are and what we do, to a depressing and likely damaging degree. It means that some people have forgotten us entirely. This is something that even libraries with the strongest, cleverest, most well-funded marketing strategies contend with, and the "image problem" remains a great threat to our profession.

We know who we are, but we don't know how to explain—or justify—our existence in a way compelling enough to once and for all shatter the stereotype. We go to the numbers and metrics—circulation statistics, cardholdership, event attendance—to show how much we matter. When we talk about the value of libraries, the way we frame our argument—or, get others to do so—matters as much as the details we are trying to get across. Measurements are important, but they don't turn heads quite the way that stories do, and the best stories are invariably tied to emotion. It's not easy, but we need to figure out a way to ascribe value to our work based on the feeling it inspires—and get our advocates to do the same.

The reason that dreaded phrase is music to my ears, each and every time I hear it, is because of the rest of the sentence that remains unspoken: "I didn't know . . . but now I do." It means you've just surprised someone. Surprise is one of the most valuable sentiments that we, as library advocates concerned with continued professional sustainability, can harness and transform into demonstrations of library value.

Here's the good news: although we must contend with outmoded sentiments in the popular imagination about what libraries are, it is also true that for many people "the library" is a place filled to the brim with magic and wonder. It makes perfect sense for us to create stories for our users to interact with, or immersive and unique experiences they will never forget. The thought of creating narrative programs "from-scratch" can seem daunting, if not impossible. They are difficult to conceive and manage, and they will stretch your creative capacities to the limit. (What was I saying about good news?) Despite the challenges they present, I promise they are entirely worth the investment of time and effort, because you will give your audience something to talk about.

In over a decade of designing programs for teens, adults, and sometimes kids in libraries, nothing I've ever worked on inspired more delight and surprise than immersive programs, most notably our Mystery Nights, and later our escape rooms. These programs are designed to challenge an audience—literally. They provoke an intense emotional response. They require communication and teamwork. They envelop you in story. They are a perfect fit for what we, as community and cultural institutions, are, but almost no one expects to find such a thing at a library.

These programs became our traditions, as treasured as storytime and long-standing book clubs, and they led our audience to truly understand what we were about—providing great experiences and building community—because we gave them a story to tell about us that transformed the "I didn't know . . ." into a sincere, passionate "Did you know?" In some of our most challenging times, when jobs were on the line, it was the stories told by our users that made all the difference. Nothing helps you justify your existence more than a compelling story, and when your advocates speak from their heart, it's not so easy to dismiss them.

Of course, when you are in the early stages of planning an original, large-scale, intricate event like an escape room, library advocacy likely isn't a prominent part of your design strategy. You will be thinking about the immediate necessities: finding space, creating puzzles, acquiring supplies, and getting the word out. That's as it should be—even the most seasoned programmer would look at the mechanics of an immersive program and feel overwhelmed. But the work you put in to your event will yield dividends that last long after the last players exit your building, because of the very *way* they will exit your building—in a state of froth.

Yes. Froth. In researching escape rooms for a workshop, I found a blog post by London-based game designer Grant Howitt that used this weird, dysphonic, wonderful word to describe a rare and valuable thing. It is a LARP term for, in a nutshell, the way people who have shared a fantastic, exhilarating experience (think, riding a roller coaster, or seeing a great concert) begin to mythologize the moment as soon as it's over. "Remember when you screamed at the top of that hill?" "Oh, and that time you almost fell dancing so hard to that song!?" Froth is the instant churning of mutual excitement that leads to the etching of memory in the mind. Even as the details fade over time, the feeling of the moment, because it is shared, lasts.[5]

If you've programmed in libraries, particularly for younger audiences, you've witnessed this. Escape rooms get really frothy, often due to the sheer surprise of a fusty, stern, serious "library" staging something that is, for all the educative spin we might slap on it, such unbridled fun. The best part of any of our escape rooms has been the very end—not when a team of players wins the game, but in the after, when we take the time to walk and talk them through it all and watch them begin to froth, or when we catch the delighted reactions of parents as they see and hear the excitement erupting from their tweens and teens at pickup time, or when we see adults allowing themselves to unabashedly celebrate victories with new friends who, only an hour previously, were tentative strangers. Escape rooms are about communication and connection, so we make sure to be present for, and a part of, the froth. We understand the value of connecting the library and the staff who have worked so diligently to produce it directly to this new memory.

And we are always planning for more. The question we hear from players at the end of every escape room session, win or lose, is "when are you going to do this again?" In that moment, it can trigger a wave of anxiety—I need to do this again?!—but there is no stronger indication that you have created something meaningful. You have given your audience something so surprising and delightful that they may come to expect, or even insist on, more of the same. Meeting demonstrated user demand is a strong justification for maintaining or, ideally, expanding your capacity to provide service. Numbers matter, but stories have a persuasive power that cannot be matched, especially when it comes to library programming.

Like any good escape room designer, I've taken a circuitous route to the point: Immersive programs are frothy, and now, more than ever, libraries need to be in the froth business. We need to give people a good story to tell about us, and a way to articulate why we matter to them. Escape rooms won't save libraries from their too-common stale image or the vicissitudes of economics, but by framing and celebrating our offerings as deeply felt experiences, designing and redesigning our services accordingly, and striving to be more cognizant of the feelings we inspire in every aspect of what we do, we just might be able to reclaim some of the puzzle pieces of "the library" image, and how our story is told by our community.

• • • • • • •

FUNDING YOUR ESCAPE ROOM

Creating and running an escape room in the library are not an incredibly costly endeavor. As discussed earlier in this chapter, the cost of most library escape rooms ranges between $0 and $150. However, you may want to come up with some creative ways to foot the bill if you are on a limited budget.

Creating a Budget

As with any other type of event you would run in the library the first thing you'll want to do when planning this event is to create a budget. The most substantial part of the cost of organizing one of these escape games is the locks, which come in all types and variations such as combination locks, key locks, alphabet locks, number locks, color locks, and so on for the player to crack. The cost of purchasing a lock kit from Breakout EDU is approximately $150 at the time of this writing. However, as discussed in chapter 4, locks can be found on Amazon for less. Once the initial investment for the locks is complete, the budget for future events such as this will be significantly less expensive. Here's a sample budget:

Expense	*Amount*
Locks	$150
Lock boxes	$ 20
Printing costs	$ 25
Props	$ 50
Refreshments	$100
Total	**$345**

Raising the Funds

There are a number of outlets that you can explore to acquire the needed funds and resources to help you run your escape game. Combining multiple sources of financing may be one way to achieve your goal.

Library Budget

Most library budgets have funds set aside for new programs. The challenge will be making the case why an escape room would be a good use of those funds. Come up with a brief elevator pitch that you can use for all these funding sources about why an escape game would be a good investment and activity for the library. For inspiration, take another look at the earlier discussion of opportunities that these types of activities present to libraries (such as passing along STEM skills, providing opportunities for developing social skills, encouraging teamwork and cooperation, etc.).

Grants

You may be seeking to create and run escape rooms on a larger scale, coordinate multiple versions of your escape room, invest in multiple lock kits, or even establish a program in which you have your younger patrons help you design your escape room like the way Nebraska's Morton-James Public Library did (as presented in chapter 3). In any of these scenarios, you will want to investigate available grants. Because escape rooms are an excellent activity for kids and young adults that can involve STEM skills, this opens a number of opportunities for applying for grants. Think about grants that fund initiatives such as makerspaces and making activities, as well as technology and computer initiatives (especially if your game involves teaching computer skills). These outlets may be suitable for your escape room program grant.

There are many different types of grant programs that may provide you with the needed funds for your escape room. These include federal grants, state government grants, corporate grants, foundation grants, library association grants, and more. If your library has a development office, speak with them to find out more about which grants may be relevant and how to apply for them. You may also seek the counsel of your state library, which can likely fill you in on local grants. Here are several grants from different sources to get you started.[6]

LIBRARY ASSOCIATIONS

Association for Library Service to Children (ALSC) grants
(www.ala.org/alsc/awardsgrants)
Young Adult Library Services Association (YALSA) grants
(www.ala.org/yalsa/awardsandgrants/yalsaawardsgrants
http://teentechweek.ning.com/page/grants-funding)

FEDERAL GOVERNMENT

Institute of Museum and Library Services (IMLS) grants
(https://www.imls.gov/grants/apply-grant/available-grants)
The Library Services and Technology Act (LSTA) grants
(https://www.imls.gov/grants/grants-states)

CORPORATIONS[7]

The Best Buy Community Grant
(https://corporate.bestbuy.com/community-grants-page/)
Cognizant's Making the Future Grant
(https://www.cognizant.com/company-overview/sustainability/educational-opportunity)

Lowe's Toolbox for Education
(http://toolboxforeducation.com)
Rockwell Collins Charitable Corporation grants
(https://www.rockwellcollins.com/Our_Company/Corporate_Responsibility/Community_Overview/Charitable_Giving.aspx)

FOUNDATIONS

W. K. Kellogg Foundation grants
(https://www.wkkf.org)
MacArthur Foundation grants
(https://www.macfound.org/info-grantseekers)
Knights Foundation grants
(https://knightfoundation.org/grants)

Donations

Don't forget about your local community! Ask your Friends of the Library group, library clubs, library staff, local businesses and organizations such as the Knights of Columbus, and so on, for donations of funds and supplies. Get everyone involved and excited about the event. Local commercial escape rooms are often eager to help out and lend props and other supplies in exchange for a little publicity for their businesses. Be sure and seek them out as well. If you are creating props and decorations that must be printed, ask your printing office or local large-format printer to donate the items.

Grassroots Fundraising

Online grassroots fundraising websites will enable you to set up a campaign for your event and raise funds from your online community. Donorschoose.org is used by educational institutions, teachers, librarians, and nonprofit organizations to raise money for programs and events. Other websites include Kickstarter, GoFundMe, and Indiegogo. Choose whichever one is best for you.

Other Resources

There are several websites and organizations that list available grants that are appropriate for libraries. Here are some of those.

YALSA Funding, Awards, and Grants List
(http://wikis.ala.org/yalsa/index.php/Funding,_Awards_and_Grants)
Scholastic Library Grants List
(www.scholastic.com/librarians/programs/grants.htm)

Demco's Library and Education Grants Database
(https://www.demco.com/goto?GRANTS)
Library Grants Blog
(http://librarygrants.blogspot.com)
EBSCO's Grants and Funding Sources for Libraries
(https://help.ebsco.com/interfaces/EBSCO_Guides/Resources_for_Librarians/Grants_Funding_Sources_for_Libraries)

NOTES

1. An account is necessary to log in to Breakout EDU, but it offers free accounts that give you access to hundreds of free games once registered.
2. Eliza Krigman, "The Latest Tools for Teaching STEM," *Video Games*, November 11, 2013, https://www.usnews.com/news/stem-solutions/articles/2013/11/11/the-latest-tool-for-teaching-stem-video-games.
3. "Escape Games: The Boredom-Crushing Classroom Tech Your Students Need," *Lock Paper Scissors*, https://lockpaperscissors.co/school-escape-games.
4. "Escape Your Thinking," *Lock Paper Scissors*, https://lockpaperscissors.co/escape-your-thinking.
5. "Frothing at the Mouth," *Look Robot*, http://lookrobot.co.uk/2012/09/11/emergent-gameplay-larp/.
6. J. Burke and E. Kroski, *Makerspaces: A Practical Guide for Librarians* (Lanham, MD: Rowman and Littlefield, 2018), 57.
7. "Awards, Grants, Stipends and Scholarships," American Library Association, January 5, 2007, www.ala.org/yalsa/awardsandgrants/yalsaawardsgrants.

3

Escape Room Activity in Libraries

ESCAPE ROOMS HAVE BEGUN TO GAIN TRACTION IN THE LIBRARY world with events hosted at major conferences, anniversary celebrations, and as stand-alone programming. In 2017, the Michigan Library Association Conference hosted an escape room as a part of their daily programming schedule during all three days of their event. They worked with a local commercial escape room, Escape Rooms Portland, Michigan (https://www.escapeportlandmi.com/) to create and organize a pop-up escape room called the *CSI: Library Murder Mystery*, an exciting whodunit game complete with chalk body outline, forensic evidence, and library book clues. Groups of up to fifteen librarians gathered together to solve the murder within an hour (see figures 3.1 to 3.3).[1]

FIGURE 3.1
Librarians listen intently for the next clue in the *CSI: Library Murder Mystery* at the 2017 Michigan Library Association Conference

FIGURE 3.2
Librarians work in teams to piece together the parts of the puzzle

The 2017 American Association of School Librarians (AASL) National Conference also featured an escape room as one of its main attractions in its exhibit hall. Also in 2017, the ALA GameRT hosted an "Escape to the Library" preconference workshop event at the ALA Annual Conference.

FIGURE 3.3
A library stamp is mulled over as the possible key to the mystery

LIBRARY ESCAPE ROOMS

Escape rooms are being hosted as a part of library programming at many libraries, including the sixteen whose escape rooms are described below. Here is what they're doing.

CASE STUDIES

TWEEN PIRATE AND ZOMBIE ESCAPE ROOMS

This case study is based on an interview
with tween and teen librarian Meghin Roberts.

Library:	Flower Memorial Library (Watertown, New York)
URL:	www.flowermemoriallibrary.org
Audience:	Tweens (ages ten to thirteen)
Estimated Number of Attendees:	fifteen (2016), nineteen (over two sessions—2017)
Number of Staff Needed:	one
Time Limit:	1 hour
Number of Players Limit:	Fifteen per session
Cost of the Event:	One-time cost of $120.13, all supplies are reusable for all future escape rooms

Tween and teen librarian Meghin Roberts designed her own pirate and zombie-themed escape rooms to engage tweens and encourage teamwork in her library. She started from scratch by first creating the theme and backstory and then deciding how many locks she would utilize. To plan her room, she created a color-coded flowchart assigning each lock and associated clue their own colors. She included red herrings and props to be used in the rooms along the sidebar of her charts. Meghin was able to repurpose everything except the themed decorations from the pirate room she created for use in the zombie game she designed. For the zombie room, she swapped out the pirate treasure in the locked box for vials of zombie cure and printed out Centers for Disease Control posters for the walls.

Both rooms relied heavily on locks including key, alphabet, number, picture, and directional locks. Each of these locks was placed on a hasp and the goal of the room was to unlock each one to reveal the treasure (or cure). Her puzzles included codes, a pigpen cypher, riddles, black-light puzzles, mazes, Dewey Decimal numbers, and dice.

> Always bring your spare keys into the room with you because no matter how much you test something there's always a chance a lock will just not work.

Meghin's rooms were run three times and two out of the three games were completed successfully, with the third game group nearly finishing the final lock as the timer ran out. According to Meghin, the smaller groups had a higher success rate with the puzzles and tended to work better together than the larger groups. In all, the programs garnered positive responses from library patrons and drew tweens that don't regularly visit the library.

> Everyone in the room needs to collaborate and discuss different solutions for the puzzles. I've noticed that the teams that have the most organized communication are the most successful. ■

LIBRARY LOCKDOWN
An Escape Room Designed by Kids

This case study is based on an interview with Jennifer Thoegersen, data curation librarian at University of Nebraska-Lincoln.

Library:	Morton-James Public Library (Nebraska City, Nebraska)
URL:	http://morton-jamespubliclibrary.com
Audience:	Project: kids; playing the room: community
Estimated Number of Attendees:	200
Number of Staff Needed:	One to run the room; approximately ten staff and volunteers worked on the project.
Time Limit:	60 minutes
Number of Players Limit:	Ten
Cost of the Event:	Financed by a $7,500 grant; free to play

Rasmus Thoegersen, the former director of the Morton-James Public Library, along with Jennifer Thoegersen, a data curation librarian at the University of Nebraska-Lincoln, worked with a group of three dozen children to create an escape room at the Morton-James Public Library. After receiving a Curiosity Creates grant from the Association for Library Service to Children (ALSC), the library organized this exciting kids' program to run every Saturday for sixteen weeks, during which time participants aged eight to thirteen dreamed up the Lab of Dr. Morton McBrains as their setting for a zombie-themed escape room. Once completed, the room was open to the public for more than six months.

> The kids who built the room loved it, and the community responded very well.

They designed their puzzles from scratch; however, they used online resources and riddle/puzzle books to inform their challenges. Their escape game incorporated riddles and codes, hidden items, locks, hidden text, and a computer program. A robot maze was also designed by the kids as a part of the room. For this puzzle, the organizers purchased the programmable robots Dot and Dash with a portion of the grant money. The kids programmed the robots to move in certain directions according to what buttons were pressed. Once in the game, players needed to press the correct buttons on the top of Dot to navigate Dash out of the robot maze. When this was achieved, a recording was accessible on Dash, which included a much-needed lock combination.

The kid-designed escape room was very popular and well-attended and the success rate for completion very high. The room was played by school classes, local businesses, families, and groups of friends. The organizers have made the entire playbook for the escape room available online at http://digitalcommons.unl.edu/cgi/viewcontent.cgi?article=1367&context=libraryscience. ■

HUSKER HISTORY MYSTERY
A Pop-Up Escape Room

This case study is based on an interview with,
data curation librarian Jennifer Thoegersen.

Library:	University of Nebraska-Lincoln Libraries
URL:	https://libraries.unl.edu
Audience:	College students
Estimated Number of Attendees:	Approximately fifty
Number of Staff Needed:	Ten worked on the room
Time Limit:	20 minutes
Number of Players Limit:	Six
Cost of the Event:	Approximately $125

This single-day pop-up escape room was designed as an outreach event by data curation librarian Jennifer Thoegersen and social sciences librarian Erica DeFrain. Its theme was time travel. It included historical facts about the university campus that not only entertained, but also educated players. Approximately ten staff members helped build the escape room out of an unused study room in the library, and another dozen helped test it out before it was open to the public.

> Definitely, definitely test the room with several groups.

The project team met weekly to brainstorm and work on designing puzzles approximately six weeks before opening. The game's challenges included riddles, secret codes, hidden text, locks, and a safe to crack, all within the twenty-minute time limit. The room had only a 60-percent success rate for those who escaped, but nonetheless received enthusiastic feedback from all who played the room, including those who didn't beat it. The organizers have made the entire playbook for the escape room available online at: https://unl.app.box.com/v/escape. ■

STAFF DEVELOPMENT DAY
Team Building Escape Room

This case study is based on an interview with librarian Susan Mythen.

Library:	Florida State College at Jacksonville
URL:	www.fscj.edu
Audience:	College Library and Learning Commons staff (librarians, library assistants, tutors, managers, and administrators)
Estimated Number of Attendees:	Seventy
Number of Staff Needed:	Two facilitators (to lead two competing groups)
Time Limit:	30 minutes
Number of Players Limit:	No limit
Cost of the Event:	$150 for Breakout EDU lock kit

Florida State College consists of five campuses with many staff members who had never met prior to the annual Library and Learning Commons Staff Development Day dedicated to brainstorming and strategic planning. Librarian Susan Mythen and her colleagues chose to organize an escape room game as a part of the event. The library had recently purchased three Breakout EDU lock kits for circulation to faculty as well as library planning, so one of these kits was used along with a ready-made escape room game from the Breakout EDU free library.

> The escape room experience was such a good ice breaker and team-building exercise. Players from different campuses and departments worked together to solve problems and break codes.

Attendees were organized into two competing groups with a thirty-minute limit, and each successfully solved the game's riddles, hidden text puzzles, secret codes, and found the hidden key within the time allotted. Because a pre-designed game was used, the event only took an hour or two to prepare, including printing and laminating documents, finding other resources (mostly books—some used in solving the puzzles and some as decoys), taping things in place, setting the locks, and learning the scenario.

The escape room received such a positive response that the library is planning another program in the near future to promote a traveling exhibit it will be hosting. The plan is to put more customizations into this next room. One lesson learned was that thirty is not an ideal team size and the next large group game would be limited to between fifteen and twenty players.

> If you're nervous about taking the plunge and designing your own escape room, a kit is a great way to begin. You can start with a tested scenario and set of puzzles, which really takes the pressure off. Once you feel comfortable with the setup and facilitation, you can start designing your own games. That's when it gets really fun! ■

BREAKOUT!
A Training Escape Room

This case study is based on an interview with access services manager Mackenzie Morning.

Library:	Winona State University Darrell W. Krueger Library
URL:	https://www.winona.edu/library
Audience:	Circulation student workers
Estimated Number of Attendees:	Test group: three staff and one student worker; actual training: fifteen student workers
Number of Staff Needed:	One
Time Limit:	20 minutes
Number of Players Limit:	No limit
Cost of the Event:	$0—the library already had the Breakout EDU kit

Access services manager Mackenzie Morning decided to create an escape room event as a way to offer training to the library's circulation student workers. The library already owned a Breakout EDU lock kit and it was these locks that she used as the impetus for her super hero–themed Circulation Breakout game. She created all the clues and puzzles from scratch, incorporating the items regularly discussed during the start-of-the-semester training session, such as how to search for articles based on citations, the Patron Problem Report form, and their recently changed attendance policy.

> Plan on more time than you anticipate. What you the planner thinks as being easy clues are typically what trips up players.
>
> Leave time for debriefing. Go over what the answer for each of the clues and Red Herrings are so, if there is poor communication, everyone knows the correct answer to each of the pieces.

The training breakout puzzles relied heavily on black-light clues and word problems. Although the student workers did not escape within the time limit, their response was quite positive because they learned about resources and policies. Mackenzie decided that in the future she would break up the group because she learned that the large group size hindered good communication and problem-solving. She would also allow more than twenty minutes for an activity like this one. In all, she was very pleased with the results and is currently planning another Breakout training session.

> Breakout EDU is a great starting point for anyone that is interested in creating escape rooms in the library. I am thrilled with the results from our training Breakout. I normally would have just done a PowerPoint of all of the forms and updates and I would then have had to repeat myself multiple times over the course of the next few weeks, as most of the students would have tuned me out. I have not had to go over any of the material presented by the Breakout and I know from my interviews, that they did get a lot out of it. I think Breakout EDU and escape rooms in general are a great resource for training. ■

DEWEY DECIMATED

Escape Randall Library: An Academic Library Escape Room

This case study is based on an interview with first-year engagement Librarian Eva Sclippa.

Library: William Madison Randall Library at UNC Wilmington
URL: http://library.uncw.edu/escape
Audience: College students, primarily freshmen
Estimated Number of Attendees: 155

Number of Staff Needed: Ten total; two to run each session
Time Limit: 60 minutes
Number of Players Limit: Ten
Cost of the Event: Approximately $300 (some funds were donated, materials were created in-house)

> You're applying to enter the Academy of Extraordinary Research, where you'll train to become sidekicks to the League of Extraordinary Researchers. The League has devised this test of your reasoning abilities, teamwork skills, and information literacy knowledge to determine whether or not to accept you. However! Their arch nemesis has secretly infiltrated the room. There is now a live warp device setup—if you don't solve the puzzles and disarm it in 60 minutes, you'll all be vaporized!

This superhero-themed escape room was designed by first-year engagement librarian Eva Sclippa and her colleagues for outreach and instruction and also to introduce participants to the special collections room where the event was hosted.

> As far as information literacy, we saw this as a chance to reinforce certain skills and, in some cases, introduce library resources, in the context of an interactive and engaging activity.

Eva and a team made up of web and applications developer Garret Corbett, special collections library specialist Rebecca Baugnon, social sciences librarian Stephanie Crow, information technology librarian Jason Fleming, sciences librarian Peter Fritzler, and transfer student services librarian Tammy Ivins designed the room entirely from scratch with puzzles primarily based around library tools and skills. They worked to be sure that puzzles didn't block access to later ones and strove to strike the right balance between open and sequential puzzles; that is, puzzles that can be worked on at any time from the moment players enter the room, as opposed to puzzles that require items or information from earlier puzzles to be completed. They utilized a variety of puzzles including secret codes, information that needed to be deciphered, hidden text, QR codes, jigsaw puzzles, and physical tasks. The team had access to an in-house 3-D printer, which they used to assemble many of their props and puzzle elements. Their room boasted a 90 percent escape rate and received very positive assessment results.

> Be prepared for people to attempt to circumvent the structure of the room or sometimes outright cheat, and have a policy ahead of time about what you'll do if this happens.

The team did extensive outreach and marketing before the event, including designing a website (http://library.uncw.edu/escape) with event information and a registration page that they shared on social media and in the university's e-newsletter. They developed custom buttons for those who escaped, announced the top teams weekly on social media and on signs in the library, and gave out prizes such as passes to a local escape room.

The team recommends including a combination of sequential and open puzzles, scripting the clue-giving portion of the room ahead of time to supply hints to players, and testing the room multiple times before the event. ■

PRE-TEEN/TEEN ESCAPE ROOMS

This case study is based on an interview with library manager Laura Burton.

Library:	Ruth Holder Public Library (Temple, Georgia)
URL:	http://facebook.com/ruthholderlibrary
Audience:	Pre-teen/teen
Estimated Number of Attendees:	A total of approximately twenty-five for the three sessions
Number of Staff Needed:	One
Time Limit:	90 minutes
Number of Players Limit:	Ten per event; each event only ran once
Cost of the Event:	$30 dollars for all three

Library manager Laura Burton created and hosted three escape rooms for library patrons: *Locked in the Library*, in which players must find their way out of the library before a tornado hits; *Escape the Haunted Library*, which is themed around players exploring an abandoned library when ghosts lock them in; and *Find the Stolen Book*, where the librarian was a master thief who had hidden a rare book in the library and left clues for herself so that she wouldn't forget where it was. Players must find the book before the librarian returns and takes it away forever.

> The difficult part was really making sure that the clues were tricky enough that they wouldn't solve them in seconds and be done in 20 minutes, but not so tricky that they couldn't solve them at all!

Because she didn't have a budget for a kit, Laura designed all her locks and puzzles from scratch using items on-hand. Her challenges consisted of rhyming couplets, Dewey Decimal puzzles to find books, black-light puzzles, and a text maze. She recommends using the website Festisite as a resource to create text mazes (https://www.festisite.com/text-layout/maze/). Laura added to the atmosphere of the games by creating sound effects such as the National Weather Service storm warning alerts and haunted house sound effects. She also used dry ice to create "mist" in the haunted room. The response to the rooms has been extremely positive with teens signing up for multiple events. ■

ESCAPE DRACULA'S LIBRARY HIGH SCHOOL ESCAPE ROOM

This case study is based on an interview with Amy Williams, District Library Teacher.

Library:	Cerro Gordo School District #100 (Cerro Gordo, Illinois)
URL:	htttp://www.cgbroncos.org
Audience:	High school students
Estimated Number of Attendees:	Thirty
Number of Staff Needed:	One
Time Limit:	45 minutes
Number of Players Limit:	Eight per group, one group per hour
Cost of the Event:	No costs; library already owned the Breakout EDU lock kit

District library teacher Amy Williams created a horror-themed library escape room based on the Bram Stoker novel *Dracula* for high school students from scratch after hosting two of the pre-designed games from the Breakout EDU library. She based her puzzles on those she had experienced in commercial escape rooms.

> I hoped to promote problem solving and critical thinking among the students.

The room contained riddles, cyphers, locks, hidden objects, ribbon wrapped around an object to spell a word, and a diary with secret codes that led players to escape from Dracula's library. Her room has a 90 percent success rate and was very popular and encouraged students to read the book. Each of her rooms is paired with a book and are run several times per year. ■

WIZARD OF OZ, MYSTERY OF THE TITANIC FAMILY, AND ADULT ESCAPE ROOMS

This case study is based on an interview with youth services librarian Rozanna Bennett.

Library:	Dodge City Public Library (Dodge City, Kansas)
URL:	www.dcpl.info
Audience:	Kids and families for *Wizard of Oz* and teens and adults for *Titanic*
Estimated Number of Attendees:	Seventy total
Number of Staff Needed:	One
Time Limit:	1 hour each session
Number of Players Limit:	No limit, but three to twelve was the range
Cost of the Event:	$200 for supplies

> It has been rumored that the Wicked Witch of the East has faked her own death. She has brought down the house of Gale upon her head in hopes of escaping the evil clutches of her sister the Wicked Witch of the West. It is your mission to find proof that she is truly dead before the Wicked Witch of the West gets to the ruby shoes! As Dorothy did, so long ago, start on the yellow brick road.

This beginner-level, family-oriented escape game was designed by youth services librarian Rozanna Bennett, who has designed a total of three escape rooms for her library. Her first room was for a summer reading program and her most recent was a Titanic-themed room geared for more advanced, adult players.

> White Star Line is under fire. It is believed that Bruce Ismay, manager of the White Star Line, is at fault. How else can it be explained that he survived, when so many women and children perished? Your mission is to find his testimony and evidence to prove that neither the White Star Line nor Bruce Ismay is at fault (*Mystery of the Titanic Family*).

All her rooms were created from scratch. She recommends beginning with a theme, identifying which locks you want to use, and then designing puzzles. Her challenges consisted of hidden text, codes, locks, UV/black-light puzzles, crossword, word, Sudoku, and jigsaw puzzles.

> Designing a game works easiest if you work backwards. Find the objective or mission that you want them to complete. Hide it, then go backwards from there, taking each clue and item at once.

She ran her Wizard of Oz and Titanic rooms simultaneously in two rooms equipped with cameras, which enabled her to watch players from her laptop to see when they were stumped and requested clues.

For future rooms, she would stagger the start times so that both wouldn't begin and end at the same time, which would allow her to dedicate more time to each group. Her rooms had a 90 percent escape rate and have been so popular that she will be running two rooms one weekend every month going forward. ■

ESCAPE THE ROOM
An Unlock the Box Event

This case study is based on an interview with youth librarian Alec Gramm.

Library:	Tippecanoe County Public Library (Lafayette, Indiana)
URL:	http://tcpl.lib.in.us
Audience:	The general public, ages 10 and up
Estimated Number of Attendees:	Twenty-four
Number of Staff Needed:	Two
Time Limit:	20 minutes
Number of Players Limit:	Eight to ten
Cost of the Event:	Less than $10

> Eccentric millionaire Madam Vivian Aldi who, having no immediate heir, sought to find which of her extended relatives were able to solve her puzzles (that she loved so dearly) in one of her favorite rooms from her home, the Room of Seasons. As it is a bit impractical to move a literal room from location to location, the essence of the room was taken and set up in different locations for her relatives to try and solve the puzzles. Her most trusted assistant hosted the event and monitored the efforts of the challenge-takers during the trial.

Youth librarian Alec Gramm designed this escape event from scratch using items from the library's programming closet, in the hope of fostering creative thinking, problem-solving, and team-building among library patrons. He also played the host, Madam Aldi's trusted assistant Mr. Ree, in the scenario while another staff member greeted players and debriefed them after the game.

His puzzles included hidden patterns, riddles, hidden numbers, hidden text, and several red herrings. The object of his room was to solve a series of challenges to unlock several locks that held a box shut rather than to escape the room as many other events require. Although the response was positive, Alec would extend the time limit for the room in the future as players found the 20-minute limit difficult.

> *TIPS FOR EXECUTION*—Don't be afraid to give hints, make the hints a part of the puzzle, and stick to your theme. ■

ESCAPE ROOMS WITHIN LARGER EVENTS

This case study is based on an interview with
Tegan Mannino, cataloger and circulation supervisor.

Library:	Monson Free Library (Monson, Massachusetts)
URL:	https://monsonlibrary.com
Audience:	Adults
Estimated Number of Attendees:	Average of forty to fifty players
Number of Staff Needed:	One or two
Time Limit:	30 to 45 minutes
Number of Players Limit:	Six to eight
Cost of the Event:	$50 to $100

Tegan Mannino, cataloger and circulation supervisor at the Monson Free Library, has developed several escape games including *American Centurions, Curtain Call, Cruel Summer, The Missing Time Turner,* and *Remedial Potions,* which have been run in conjunction with larger Live Action Role Playing (LARP) games in her library and other places.

> Players really got into it, reacting in character to being trapped in the room, and incorporating this into the larger event experience.

A LARPer and long-time gamer herself, Tegan developed her escape rooms from scratch in modules that would provide those who solved separate side quests with bonus items that would give them a leg up within the larger LARPs that they were immersed in. She started with her narrative and puzzle ideas and then worked backwards to design her first rooms, which she then repurposed for later games with different themes. Tegan used her experience playing escape room games to implement a wide variety of puzzle types in her rooms, including a hidden word on a mirror; transparent overlay sheets that revealed critical information; tangram puzzles; riddles, hidden numbers; puzzle boxes; a dowel puzzle in which dowels of different lengths had to be slotted into different depth holes to stand at equal heights; a hollow book; hidden images; red-reveal, black-light, weight, and word puzzles; and hidden objects. She offers this advice when designing your own rooms: test your puzzles, double-check your locks, and be aware that tangram puzzles have more than one solution.

> There are lots of things in a library which are not a part of the escape room that will catch the player's attention and that they will fixate on as clues. You need to determine if you want there to be failures or if you want to nudge people into completion outside of a set number of tips.

The escape rooms in both the LARPs and in the library were very popular. Tegan has since purchased a Breakout EDU kit and plans to acquire a second one for her future escape games. ■

ESCAPE THE FAIRY TALE
A Multiple Room Kids Escape Game

This case study is based on an interview with children's librarians Lisa O'Shaughnessy and Marissa Lieberman.

Library:	East Orange Public Library (East Orange, New Jersey)
URL:	www.eopl.org
Audience:	Kids, third to seventh grade
Estimated Number of Attendees:	Twenty
Number of Staff Needed:	Two
Time Limit:	Ten minutes per room for a total of 20 minutes per session
Number of Players Limit:	Ten per session
Cost of the Event:	$100

> You are on adventure through fairy land when you come upon the home of the three bears. Goldilocks, however, has already been through the house and messed everything up. She has locked you inside but has left clues for you to find the code to open the lock that will let you escape before the three bears return.

Children's librarians Lisa O'Shaughnessy and Marissa Lieberman split their large programming room in half and created two connecting escape rooms from scratch. After completing the first escape room, participants entered the second room. When they completed the second room, they were able to enter back into the library, completing *Escape the Fairy Tale*. When each group escaped back to the library, they were given signs to hold up for a group photo.

> The goal of Escape the Fairy Tale was to bring fairy tales to life and promote literacy in an engaging environment.

Players were greeted in each room by a fairy narrator who guided them through the room if they ran into problems. The librarians felt that with children as their audience, this framing device and assistance would work both to enhance their experience and ensure a fun and successful program. And they were correct—their success rate was 100 percent for their rooms.

> You have entered Rumpelstiltskin's world where a young woman was forced to spin straw into gold. As she could not, Rumpelstiltskin appeared to help her and in return for his help she promised him her first-born child. After a year and a day, he returned and told the queen if she could guess his name she could keep her child. The queen could not, and Rumpelstiltskin escaped with the child. The knights are out searching for Rumpelstiltskin and hidden all over are clues to help you escape and help find the child. Start digging.

Participants were immersed in a fairytale realm and made their way from the cottage of the three bears that Goldilocks happened upon to Rumpelstiltskin's world, which was separated into two spaces—the miller's daughter's room equipped with a spinning wheel and a pile of hay and the throne room. Riddles, hidden text, and alphabet locks were used in each room to challenge players. The game designers enhanced the experience by adding a soundtrack, dramatic lighting, and dressing up like fairies, as well as following a script to introduce each story. They also recorded the game via webcams for the library's archive. They recommend considering your target age group when designing puzzles and to test out sample clues on prospective players ahead of time. ■

MUSEUM HEIST
A Collaboration with a Local Escape Room

This case study is based on an interview with Jim Curry, MLS student at University of North Carolina at Chapel Hill and teen librarian Tara Smith.

Library:	Charlotte Mecklenburg Library ImaginOn Branch
URL:	https://www.imaginon.org
Audience:	Preteens and teens (10 to 18)
Estimated Number of Attendees:	First session = thirty participants over a week and a half. Second session = twenty-one in one night
Number of Staff Needed:	First session = three. Second session = one or two
Time Limit:	20 to 30 minutes
Number of Players Limit:	Six to eight
Cost of the Event:	$40 to $50 per room

For their first Museum Heist themed escape room, Jim Curry, an MLS student at the University of North Carolina at Chapel Hill, and his team, which included lead teen librarian Tara Smith, Teen Loft manager Kelly Czarnecki, and teen services specialist Lillian Mayer, partnered with local escape room business The Box. Their gamemasters came in to the library to discuss their process of design, assess the space, and give advice about how to adapt a game to the age group the library was targeting. The Box staff invited the Teen Librarian staff to visit their business to play the games for free to get inspiration for puzzles and challenges. They also received assistance from Travis Sanford of the Spartanburg County Public Libraries who was generous enough to share his planning resources. They based some of the puzzles in their *Museum Heist* escape room on puzzles in Sanford's rooms.

By their second escape room they were confident in their abilities and designed a game to promote their Teen Community Read, Nicola Yoon's *The Sun Is Also a Star*. They reproduced scenes from the book to serve as New York locations for teens to visit and experience.

> You can make a really good room on a limited budget. Compensate with a strong narrative and cohesive puzzle structure. Use sound and decoration to create atmosphere.

They utilized letter locks, word puzzles, black-light puzzles, and a woodblock puzzle that was made in their makerspace. They created a video trailer to promote the room and an introductory video to immerse players and explain the rules and scenario.

> Have staff test it beforehand but be prepared to lower your already "easy" room for teens. ■

A CLOCK IS TICKING TEEN ESCAPE ROOM

This case study is based on an interview with teen services librarian Thomas Maluck.

Library:	Richland Library (Columbia, South Carolina)
URL:	www.richlandlibrary.com
Audience:	Teens, with library staff helping test the room
Estimated Number of Attendees:	Twelve total
Number of Staff Needed:	Two
Time Limit:	One hour per session
Number of Players Limit:	Six per session
Cost of the Event:	$34 for lockboxes, plus office and personal props

> Secret agent, Vivian Darkbloom has planted a bomb in the city and it will explode in one hour. She has been operating out of a library meeting room, and it is your job to investigate for clues. You must find a code phrase to transmit to one of her operatives as a signal to deactivate the bomb. The clock is ticking and there's only one way out. Can you and your team complete this mission?

Teen services librarian Thomas Maluck and the staff of the Richland County Library designed an exciting escape room filled with intrigue. It was inspired by their experiences at Escape Plan Columbia as well as a professional development event which included librarians Donald Dennis and Stephanie Frey from Georgetown County Library in South Carolina. They used an Excel spreadsheet to plan their room, plotting out all the keys, clues, and locks, as well as where each figured into the overall room.

Their puzzles included hidden keys, clues that combined to form a message, photos that referenced locations on a map, a clock that held a clue to a password, a message taped to a Jenga block, and clues that referenced a date on a calendar (which was filled with red herrings). They worked with their

Technology Department to set up an iPhone to unlock with a specific password, and to have background images on the lock and home screens to serve as clues.

> Make the escape room you're comfortable making. As long as participants are solving puzzles to escape a room, you have made an escape room. Don't let professional, sprawling setups intimidate you.

The room had a very positive response although participants weren't able to solve it. Based on this experience, Thomas shares the following advice.

- Open with an icebreaker to get everyone acquainted and comfortable with each other so they can get over any initial social discomfort and start combining clues.
- Give crystal-clear instructions to players at the beginning of the event about the boundaries of the room and what is considered "in play."
- Consider a policy of "each solution works only once" to reduce redundancy and frustration for players.
- Let players make mistakes and work out problems on their own, but don't be afraid to review your hint system if you think they're struggling.
- Provide ample resources for taking notes, whether white boards, sticky notes, notebooks, or all three.
- Count on your players messing up. Something that seems obvious to you and your testers will get misinterpreted by someone else.
- Commemorate the occasion for the players with photos and escape signs.
- Send frequent reminders! Someone who seems excited and committed at registration time may forget or disregard it. ■

HIGH SCHOOL ESCAPE ROOMS

This case study is based on an interview with Library Media Specialist Melissa Lopes.

Library:	Windsor Locks Public Schools (Windsor Locks, Connecticut)
Audience:	High school students, grades 9 through 12
Estimated Number of Attendees:	Ninety per week
Number of Staff Needed:	One

Time Limit: None
Number of Players Limit: Fourteen per session
Cost of the Event: None. The library already owned the Breakout EDU kits

Library media specialist Melissa Lopes creates custom-designed escape games for a wide array of subject areas such as algebra, pre-calculus, forensics, energy, and works of literature such as *Othello, Of Mice and Men,* and *The Odyssey,* based on teacher requests.

> The participation response has been great. The teachers enjoy them, as well as the students. Students actually go to the teachers and ask them to ask me to make them for the class.

Puzzles and challenges include crossword puzzles, ciphers, hidden numbers, black-light puzzles, puzzle pieces created in the school's tech room, picture puzzles, and matching patterns. Melissa starts off by developing the theme and narrative, decides on the final puzzle, and then works backwards from there. She finds props at home, in the drama department, and around the school. She monitors players from a window inside the escape room space.

> I really think the students have developed a stronger sense of communication, collaboration, and critical thinking skills. ■

FOUR ESCAPE ROOMS WITH ADULT APPEAL

This case study is based on an interview with youth services librarian Marissa Bucci and, outreach services specialist Nicole Scherer.

Libraries: The Ferguson Library (Stamford, Connecticut) and Fairfield (Connecticut) Public Library
URL: https://fergusonlibrary.org and http://fairfieldpubliclibrary.org
Audience: Sessions are targeted for various audiences, including families, kids, tweens, teens, adults, and librarians
Estimated Number of Attendees: Over the course of four different games, Fairfield = 250 and Ferguson= 45
Number of Staff Needed: At least two who understand the game and how to run it.

Time Limit:	1 hour per session, with approximately 5 minutes before the session for introduction and rules, and approximately ten minutes after for debrief and walk-throughs
Number of Players Limit:	Ten, unless for a family session, in which case fourteen
Cost of the Event:	$100

Youth services librarian Marissa Bucci teamed up with outreach services specialist Nicole Scherer to create four exciting escape room games for their library patrons. Games included *Escape the Attic,* in which participants were tasked with finding a map to a secret island hidden in grandma's messy attic, *Escape from Malfoy Manor,* in which players need to find a horcrux in order to save the world; *Escape the Arctic,* which involves foiling a mad scientist by locating the chemical formula of an antidote; and *(Re)Build A Better World,* a scenario in which players find themselves locked in the office of a corrupt scientist along with a hidden formula for cold fusion; to win the game, participants must find the formula and unlock the door code in time.

Their goal was to encourage teamwork and collaboration by designing the game in such a way that these were necessary to win. They also wanted to engage another segment of the community by offering adult sessions designed to demonstrate to people who may not normally use the library that it offers much more than books and storytimes.

> It's easy to fall in love with your own cleverness when you're designing games like this, but we think that if your ultimate goal is to give everyone an unforgettable experience, it should end with a celebratory feeling. That said, we do keep a public leaderboard that all teams see before the game begins, so that feeling of competitiveness is still in the air.

Marissa and Nicole designed their rooms from scratch based on their experience creating original live-action games for their teen audiences—their most popular annual event is an after-hours haunted house/library catalog-centric scavenger hunt—so they had some background in clue-making and timing. They began with the stories, and then started thinking of different clue types that could be made to fit within the context of the story so that everything in a game would feel connected to its narrative. They gathered the items needed to make clues, kept everything organized as they went with index cards, and then tested out the completed games. From there, they edited them by changing elements as needed depending on the results of the test groups.

They utilized a large variety of puzzle types in their rooms, including secret codes for which the decoders were hidden, text overlays, invisible ink writing, combination locks and keyed lockboxes, audio clues (using a song with a significant lyric that repeated over and over again during the game), mechanical clues that required putting parts together to reveal clues.

> These programs are intimidating—but worth every bit of effort you put into them! Take some time to look around online for ideas on puzzles and clues and reach out to other library staff who have done Escape Rooms (like us!) and ask for help.

The success rate of their room was close to 99 percent. They made a conscious decision that they wanted everyone to win, so that meant some teams got some extra help in the form of clues and gentle prodding towards the solutions needed to get them there. The participant response was overwhelmingly positive. Players truly immersed themselves in the game and came out of the experience talking about certain elements as though they were real. (This was also seen in the way that players interacted with the game, referring to characters and speculating about their motives.) Additionally, several adult participants reported they would be more likely to come to the library if it offered more events like this. The responses showed that people were discovering new ways to engage with the library, and that they were excited about it!

Marissa and Nicole offer these tips to librarians creating their own games:

1. Make sure you leave enough time to reset in between sessions. It's better to spread out sessions too much than be scrambling. This will also minimize mistakes by having enough time to check work.
2. Make sure that at least two other staff members or volunteers understand the workings of the game and know basic troubleshooting techniques.
3. Keep your red herrings to a minimum. They may seem like cool, ambiance-enhancing elements, but all the ephemera makes resetting more tedious and may slow down your groups too much.
4. Test runs are extremely important. Test runs with staff help you work out kinks and learn what puzzles are too easy or difficult. Because it's simple to get caught up in your own head while designing a game, it's important to have trusted colleagues give honest feedback before you unveil your game to the public.
5. Don't hesitate to edit the game as it goes along if it will improve player experience.
6. Get coworker buy-in and promotional support. If your colleagues can't explain what you are doing to potential attendees, you're likely losing the chance to get them into the program. Make them your test group if you can—they'll give you feedback and be able to explain the game to players.

7. Make sure you take time with players after the game is over to show them how it all works, what they might have missed, and to celebrate their successes.

Nicole has created an escape room manual, which is available at https://libraryladynicole.com/programs/escape-room.

■■■■■

EXAMPLES OF LIBRARY ESCAPE ROOM GAMES

There are twelve free library-related escape room games available on Breakout EDU (https://platform.breakoutedu.com/category/user-generated-library). Here are descriptions of three of them.[2]

The Wonderful World of Dewey

https://platform.BreakoutEDU.com/game/wonderfulworlddewey

This is a 45-minute game recommended for middle school students that can be run with an entire class at one time. The game teaches students about the Dewey Decimal system and how to use the library. You can find the entire game online, complete with set-up instructions, lock combinations, all the game resources and documents, and a set-up video walkthrough. Here's the introductory narrative.

> The library is one of the most important places in the school. Here you will not only be able to find magical books to read for pleasure, but you will be able to find interesting information here. This is also a great place to develop good approaches to learning and to become good at understanding information. Looking around you may notice that lots of the books have numbers on the side of them. This is called the Dewey Decimal Number and is used to organize the books using the Dewey Decimal Classification System. You may also see that the books are lined up in order number and not in alphabetical order. Why do you think this might be?
>
> Today you are going to have to use your information retrieval skills, as well as logic to learn more about this classification system. You will have to answer questions, solve puzzles and work together to answer a series of clues, which will lead you to unlocking boxes and eventually unlocking the library skills achievement!

Locked in the Library

https://platform.BreakoutEDU.com/game/locked-in-the-library

This is meant to be a 35-minute escape room game that teaches students how to search for books using the Follet Destiny online catalog; however, this can be modified for your own library's catalog. All the print resources and digital files are available online along with a walkthrough video. Here's the introduction to the game.

> Last night the Secret Association of Library Teachers, or SALT, had their monthly meeting here in our library. (I guess it isn't much of a secret!) When I came in today I noticed a few strange things. There's this large box with all of these padlocks on it and these envelopes. There's a note too.
>
> > Dear Library Teacher,
> >
> > We left you a treasure, but you can only have it if your students can unlock all of the locks. To unlock the locks your students will need to prove their mastery of Destiny. Please put your students in three teams. Give each team an envelope. You have 35 minutes. We will be watching. Begin.
> >
> > Respectfully,
> >
> > SALT

Library Skills Save the Day

https://platform.BreakoutEDU.com/game/library-skills-save-the-day

This 30-minute library orientation escape room is designed to teach an entire class of students how to develop skills using different library resources, including print books using the Dewey Decimal system, QR codes, the library website, and more. The set-up walkthrough video, all game resources including printable documentation, lock combinations, and more can be found online. Here's the introduction.

> Welcome to ____________________ [insert your library name], thank goodness you're here. I really need your help. Evil Dr. Nirb Egap has just hacked into the Google servers and is threatening to shut down Google completely. We all use Google on a regular basis and love and depend on it, so we can't let him shut it down. However, the evil doctor, while he is evil, realizes that we often

> forget about resources at our fingertips. This locked box contains the code to counteract Dr. Egap's evil plan. In order to break into the box to retrieve the code you must work together and demonstrate your library skills. You have 30 minutes to complete your mission. Good luck.

At the time of this writing, nine additional free library-related escape rooms can be found on the Breakout EDU platform along with eight more for those who subscribe to the platform. The additional eight have been designed by the experts at Breakout EDU and consist of titles like *Cracking the Code, Trapped Between Pages,* and *Mix Up in the Library: A Tale of Many Genres.*

Harry Potter Library Escape Room

www.programminglibrarian.org/programs/harry-potter-escape-room

This excellent 30-minute Harry Potter–themed library escape room was designed by the Laramie County (Wyoming) Library System's Robin Papaleka, an adult programming specialist, and Anna McClure, a digital marketing specialist. This program cost less than $100 and to date over four hundred people have played the game. Detailed instructions including an image gallery and digital files are available online. Here's the introduction.

> Hello. You have been given detention by Professor Vector. It is rumored that the last student that was given detention by Professor Vector was forgotten in her office while the Quidditch loving professor enjoyed herself at a Quidditch game. The poor Slytherin boy was never seen again.
>
> You must escape Professor Vector's office, so the same fate does not befall you. You have a half an hour to solve all the puzzles. You do not need to rip anything or take anything off the walls. You will be given no hints. If you do not complete all of the puzzles before the 30 minutes are up or if you come out of the room before solving all the puzzles, you will lose.

There are countless other library-related escape rooms available online and a search of Google or Pinterest will return many results that will get you started with inspiring scenarios and walkthroughs. Here are some useful search terms that can be plugged in along with or independent of the term "library": "escape games," "live action games," "escape rooms," and "mystery games."

Twenty-Five Different Puzzles Types Used by Library Escape Rooms

1. Riddles
2. Ciphers and secret codes
3. Black-light puzzles
4. Hidden objects
5. Hidden text
6. Hidden numbers
7. Crossword puzzles
8. Word puzzles
9. Sudoko
10. Jigsaw puzzles
11. Matching patterns
12. Mazes
13. Dewey Decimal number/call number puzzles
14. Maps
15. Mirrors
16. Rhyming couplets
17. Dice
18. QR codes
19. Physical tasks
20. Library tools and skills puzzles
21. Wrapping ribbon around an object to spell a word
22. Hollow books
23. Red reveal puzzles
24. Weight puzzles
25. Wooden block puzzles

Popular Themes Used in Library Escape Rooms

Pirates
Zombies
Time travel
Shakespeare
Super Heroes
Storms
Ghosts
Heists
Bombs
Vampires
Works of Literature
Movies
Fairy Tales
History
Math
Science

NOTES

1. Escape Rooms Portland Michigan, https://www.escapeportlandmi.com.
2. A free account is required to log in and access this and other free games on Breakout EDU.

PART II

How to Create, Organize, and Run Eleven Project Types

4

How to Host a Pre-Designed Escape Room Event

NOW THAT WE'VE HAD A LOOK AT HOW LIBRARIES ARE INCORPO-rating these engaging and educational events into their programming, let's turn our attention to how you can get started hosting these events in your own library. This chapter will walk you through how to create, organize, and run a basic escape room game.

Planning an escape room game in your library is an exciting undertaking for both library staff and patrons, and some libraries are now involving their patrons in the planning and creation process. This is a chance to add mystery and magic to your library programming while also passing along valuable learning outcomes and providing team-building scenarios. Although new, there are already plenty of pre-designed escape room kits for you to harvest and tailor to your own needs. The best part is, you don't need to have any game development experience in order to host one of these ready-made events. Premade kits come with detailed instructions for organizers that specify everything from number of players per event to lock combinations. The following is a blueprint for what's involved with hosting an event with an escape room kit.[1]

ESCAPE ROOM KITS

Breakout EDU

https://www.BreakoutEDU.com

Breakout EDU is an immersive learning games platform founded by a team of educators who brought a group of students to an escape room and later wondered "why isn't learning in the classroom this much fun?" With that in mind, they decided to try to change that traditional experience through a locked box instead of a locked room. They wanted to design a way to not only provide a subject-based learning opportunity, but also to teach students how to work with a diverse group of peers on a project while developing problem-solving skills organically. As students work to solve the series of critical-thinking puzzles needed to crack these escape rooms, they learn how to change gears and to try something else when they fail to open a lock, rather than quit in frustration. And after two years in business, Breakout EDU has built quite a community of educators and librarians through word-of-mouth alone.[2]

Breakout EDU offers a kit of resettable locks and boxes for use in their (or any other) escape room games. The kit includes two lockable boxes, a hasp, and multiple types of locks including an alphabet multilock, a directional multilock, a three-digit lock, a four-digit lock, and a key lock, as well as alternate color, shape, and number wheels for the multilocks. The kit also contains an invisible ink black-light pen for writing clues that can only be seen with a UV light (which is also included in the kit), a red lens viewer, a thumb drive, hint cards, and a set of reflection cards for discussion afterward. With this single $150 kit, escape room planners can run any of the 450+ games available on the platform. The kit also includes premium access to Breakout EDU's platform for a year, which unlocks even more games designed by the folks at Breakout EDU.

Whether or not the kit is purchased, Breakout EDU provides free access to hundreds of escape room scenarios that have been designed by educators and librarians. With free registration, users can create accounts and browse through categories including math, science, literature, social studies, languages, library skills, and more, and view and access detailed instructions for educational games such as *The Wonderful World of Dewey, Locked in the Library,* and *Back to the Future.* Each game scenario contains everything you need to run the escape room including information on recommended age ranges, content areas, ideal group sizes, story backgrounds, and set-up instructions, as well as lock combinations, a link to a Google Drive with all the game resources including printable documents and graphics, and a video that gives an overview of the game.

One fast and easy way to organize an escape room event is to order a Breakout EDU lock kit, choose an escape room scenario from their website that suits your desired learning outcomes, and follow the instructions. This would be the least-hassle entry into running escape room games in the library. However, game organizers have many additional choices to browse and may even choose a hybrid approach to tweak an existing escape room game to better fit their needs.

Lock Paper Scissors

https://lockpaperscissors.co

Lock Paper Scissors provides printable escape room kits for both kids and adults, such as *The Lost Mummy, Escape Room Z,* and *Hack the Room.* Each self-contained kit costs $19.99 and comes with all the printables needed for the event, including slickly designed marketing posters and invitations, a PowerPoint file that organizers can customize before printing, and even a Spotify playlist for background music.

Thinkfun Board Games

www.thinkfun.com/escapetheroom

Thinkfun, an educational game manufacturer, has created a series of escape room board games including *Mystery at the Stargazer's Manor* and Secret of *Dr. Gravely's Retreat.* Priced at $21.99, these prepackaged escape room games come complete with all instructions and game items as well as access to supplemental items on the Thinkfun website, including printable invitations, Pandora and Spotify playlists, costume suggestions, and reference photos. These and other board game options are discussed in detail in chapter 11.

Escape Empire

https://escapeempire.com

Escape Empire designs escape room packages aimed at commercial escape room businesses. It features single-room and multi-room packs that include everything from website copy to diagrams, printables, parts lists, hints lists, and more. At around $400 each, these kits may be expensive for libraries, but they are a good source of inspiration.

Pinterest Boards

https://www.pinterest.com

There are many boards on Pinterest that feature pins with escape room scenarios. A search for "escape room ideas," "escape room games" or "escape room ideas libraries" will return hundreds of related pins with downloadable scenarios.

The first step to hosting one of these events is to choose one of these already existing scenarios and start printing out your game pieces and preparing your props according to the provided instructions. If you want more control over your game, you may choose to follow the next program idea and design your escape room from scratch.

Putting Together a Lock Kit

If you decide to forego the Breakout EDU kit, you can easily assemble your own lock kit to match the escape room scenario that you've chosen. A quick search of Amazon for these terms will get you started with everything you need:

- Directional locks
- Padlocks and hasps
- Alphabet locks
- Three-digit locks
- Four-digit locks
- Color locks
- Bike locks

You might also look around for unique locks that would fit your time period or theme. Amazon searches for "unique locks," "antique locks" or "pirate locks" each return some very interesting possibilities. Whatever your theme, try out a related search to see if there is a matching lock or lockable item.

While you're searching, you'll want to look around for some lock boxes for your different puzzles, or you can make your own lockables by purchasing cable cords or seals to wrap around objects and lock them up. Pay close attention to how large the latches are on your lockable items to be sure that your locks will fit, or vice versa. However, if your latches are too narrow, you could also use cable cords for them. Interesting and affordable lock boxes as well as inexpensive safes can be found on both Amazon and eBay. A search for "lockable box," "lockable chest," or "lockable bag" should bring back all the results you need.

Don't forget about technology when designing your game. You can include smartphones and tablets that contain clues in the form of recorded videos, documents, or even wallpaper. These devices, along with USB flash drives, can be set to lock and reveal their vital clues only when players find the correct combinations to unlock them.

MARKETING YOUR ESCAPE ROOM

Just because you build it doesn't mean they'll come, especially if you don't get the word out. You'll want to take full advantage of the printable and graphic files that come with your escape room game to display intriguing posters and scatter invitations on tables throughout the library. You'll also want to post about it on your library website, Twitter account, and Facebook page. Your marketing materials should specify how to sign up for a specific time slot, because you don't want fifty people showing up to play all at once. Organize a registration sheet for the times you'll run the game, leaving at least one hour in between escape room sessions to give yourself a chance to reset all the locks and be sure your props are back in place.

THE DAY OF THE EVENT

Once you've chosen your escape room scenario and have your locks and lockable boxes ready, the next step is to run the event. You should have detailed instructions for what's expected of the game host and should have the scene set for your game.

The Pre-Game Experience

You will need to set up a pre-game area away from your game room so that no one can overhear anything like post-game discussions by the previous group as they exit. You should also designate an area for players to leave their belongings so that they don't have to carry them around during the game. The pre-game area is where you will give all the instructions to players. You may consider dressing up in costume to match your game motif to add to the ambiance.

Before entering the escape room, read the introduction or overview of your scenario to the participants. Let them know how much time they have to solve the room, how to ask for hints, and set the scene for play. This will get everyone in the mindset of your theme and give them the parameters of the game.

During the pre-game it is important for you to explain the boundaries of your game area if it is a shared space in the library. Specify areas and objects that are out of bounds such as works of art on the walls, light fixtures, thermostats, electrical cabinets, air vents, and floor grates. This might seem obvious to you, but you would be surprised what players will attempt to dismantle while searching for a clue. Additionally, if you have absolutely anything that resembles food items or drinkable liquids such as potions, beakers with scientific experiments, and so on, you will also want to warn players not to consume them.

Gameplay

During the actual gameplay when players are engaged in solving puzzles, you as the host should be a silent observer whether you choose to remain in the room or monitor from outside. Although it will be difficult not to help players with the puzzles, it is considered a best practice to wait until a hint is requested to supply assistance. You may choose, however, to give players updates on the countdown clock a couple of times during the game so that they know how much time is remaining.

The Debriefing

Once the allotted time is up and the game has concluded, players appreciate a debriefing on what remained for them to solve if they weren't able to finish; or even if they did finish, they may enjoy a discussion of different ways they could have solved puzzles and/or any hidden items that they may have missed. This is a time for you to congratulate them on their success and/or let them know how they matched up against previous players.

Victory Photos and Props

When and if players complete all the puzzles and solve your escape room, you will want to give them a chance to take a group photo afterward. Often escape rooms will have signs that players display in the photos that say things like "We Escaped," "We Broke Out," or "We Found the Treasure." Whatever your escape room theme, be sure to have some victory signs printed out and ready for players to display in their group photos.

Resetting the Room

As previously discussed, you will want to reserve at least one hour between runs of your escape room game. During this time, you will reset all the locks in the room, replace all clues in the locked boxes and lockables, and to check every single one of your props to make sure they haven't been damaged and are back in place. If you are using any type of technology in your escape room, be sure to test that out as well. Keep an eye out for any notes left by the previous group and be sure to get rid of these. Reset your clock and you're ready to go again.

Preparing a Troubleshooting Toolbox

If it can go wrong, it just might. You always want to be ready for that eventuality. It is a good idea to prepare a toolbox that will help you troubleshoot anything that might come up during your game. Here are some recommended items:

- Bolt cutters to cut off locks
- Extra UV flashlights (if your room uses black light in puzzles)
- An extra UV pen to rewrite smeared/faded clues
- Extra keys to locks
- Extra copies of fragile props
- Extra batteries for flashlights, props, etc.

Starting off by using a ready-made escape room scenario and a Breakout EDU lock kit is the simplest and most straightforward way to jump right into hosting these types of events. However, after you've run a couple of these games, you may want to custom-design one of these rooms from scratch. Or even take a hybrid approach and start with an existing scenario and alter it to make it more tailored for your library. The next program idea will inform you about how to do just that.

NOTES

1. Jennifer Thoegersen and Rasmus Thoegersen, "Pure Escapism: Programs That Pop," *Library Journal,* July 18, 2016, https://lj.libraryjournal.com/2016/07/opinion/programs-that-pop/pure-escapism-progams-that-pop.
2. Phone interview with James Sanders, cofounder of Breakout EDU, October 24, 2017.

5

How to Design an Escape Room from Scratch

YOU MIGHT DECIDE THAT YOU WANT TO BRING AN ESCAPE ROOM to life on your own. This is an exciting process in which you develop the story, craft the puzzles, provide the clues, and guide the players through your narrative to the eventual solution of your room. Designing one of these games yourself allows you to incorporate content specific to your library, construct puzzles and challenges tailored to your own learning outcomes, and even weave in seasonal themes, specific works of literature, local history, and other custom topics. This programming idea will walk you through how you can get started designing your own escape room from square one.

TYPES OF ESCAPE ROOMS

The first thing to be aware of when designing a game like this is that there are several different organizational styles of escape rooms, each with its own benefits and drawbacks.

Linear

A linear-style game will present a sequence of puzzles for players to solve in a specific order. Each one of the puzzles presented must be solved before players can move ahead to the next. For example, in an escape room made up of multiple rooms, players will be challenged to unlock the doors to each new room before moving ahead. This type of escape room is easiest for beginner players because there's not a lot going on at the same time. There's only one puzzle to work on at any given moment. The disadvantage to this kind of room, however, is that it's optimal for very small groups such as one to three or perhaps four because only so many people can be working on one lock at a time.[1]

Nonlinear

This style game is made up of several puzzles that can all be tackled at the same time. They often provide clues for one final larger puzzle that is the closing challenge to solve the room. These types of rooms are well-suited to large groups, allowing players to break off into smaller groups to work on different puzzles, and to more experienced players. The downside to this type of room is that they can become confusing with so much going on at once, especially for novice players.[2]

Mixed

A mixed type of room has both linear and nonlinear elements to it, incorporating the benefits of each style into one. This type of room will feature a well-organized mix of both puzzles; for example, it may begin with a linear puzzle such as a locked door leading to a room filled with nonlinear challenges, which might culminate in clues for a second locked door that must be passed through to gain access to another set of nonlinear puzzles, and so on. Mixed-style rooms are suited for groups of all sizes.[3]

Scavenger Hunts

This style differs from the previously discussed rooms because it's not made up of puzzles at all, but simply requires finding objects in the room. Although the task of finding objects is often woven into escape rooms, these rooms are all about finding items. This type of room is suited for all sizes of groups but will likely not be challenging enough for veteran players.

These organizational and puzzle styles are useful to bear in mind as you begin to craft your first escape room.[4]

CONCEPTUALIZING A THEME

As you begin to brainstorm your escape room game, the first thing that you'll want to pin down is the overarching theme of the room. Will you go with something traditional like escaping from prison, breaking out of a room to flee a zombie, evading the clutches of a band of pirates, or solving a crime with Sherlock Holmes, or will you devise a theme based on local history, the library's collection, an upcoming holiday, or a well-loved film or book such as one from the Harry Potter series? The concept or theme will set the tone and environment for your entire game, so be sure you're ready to commit to it.

My library is a historic law library in New York City that owns many titles authored by, written about, or previously owned and signed by Alexander Hamilton. As well, the Founding Father is buried across the street in the graveyard at Trinity Church. I decided to make Alexander Hamilton an integral part of my escape room theme as an opportunity to highlight these items in our collection as well as pique the interest of our members.

Whatever your theme, the idea is to model your puzzles, craft your decorations, create your props, and phrase your clues in ways that are fitting for the theme, era, universe, or scenario.

DEVELOPING THE NARRATIVE

Although not all escape rooms have a consistent (or any!) narrative structure, it is a good idea to develop at least the bare bones of a flowing narrative for your game. This will help solidify your game objective in the minds of your players and add to the ambiance of the game.

This narrative will tell the story of your game. It will weave together the challenges and puzzle pieces that will ultimately solve the room. Here is where you can make the experience magical, set players off on an adventure, offer them the opportunity to become heroes (or villains), and let them experience the thrill of a movie or video game in real life.

Once you have decided on your theme, keep expanding it until you've told the story of your game. Create a short—one or two paragraphs—introduction to your game that will be read at the beginning of your escape room event, during the pre-game experience. This introduction and background narrative will guide you through the rest of the development of your game. You may even record a video to introduce players to your game. To give you an example, here is the introduction for the escape room that I designed.

The Search for Alexander Hamilton and the Missing Librarian: A Time Travel Adventure

Resident librarian, cat lover, and conspiracy theorist Addison Adley has vanished into thin air. She was last seen in the private library of Alexander Hamilton conducting research surrounding her life's work and obsession, which is her theory that founding father Alexander Hamilton did not die on July 12, 1804, as a result of his duel with Aaron Burr, but instead was an intrepid time traveler who used the incident as an opportunity to disappear to travel through the ages. Not surprisingly, the authorities are not taking this seriously. Your job is to find clues to her disappearance before the local police come in to clear the crime scene and disrupt everything. You have thirty minutes.

CREATING THE GAME

The next step in the process is to start building your game. During this phase of development, you will decide what types of puzzles you want to include, decide how many challenges there will be, how many locks will need to be unlocked to solve your room or rooms, what types of clues will be necessary to lead players to your desired outcome, and what elements you will include in your game. For a one-hour game, an average of four to six locked items within the room should suffice. You don't need to make all the puzzles difficult. Think about including a combination of easy challenges, especially at the beginning of the game, to build player confidence, incorporating more complex or drawn-out puzzles as the game moves on.

Designing your own puzzles may seem difficult at first, but there's no need to completely reinvent the wheel. There are plenty of challenges included in sample escape room scenarios available online to provide you with inspiration. You can also consider your room's theme, time period, or desired learning outcomes to inform your puzzles. Think about ways that you can weave these into the narrative and theme you've decided upon. Will you provide a hint in a handwritten journal? Will there be hidden clues in a police report? Will players hear a warning coming from a nearby radio? Each of your challenges should further immerse your players in the story line.[5]

In addition to creating your puzzles and inserting locked items into your room, you will also want to create some pointers that will lead players along the path to the solutions. You can achieve this by color-coding those clues that lead to the same puzzle or you can emphasize the right path for players by providing redundant clues. Spread clues and puzzle pieces throughout your room; however, if you're worried a clue might be missed, think about ways that you can make it more obvious. For example, if you have highlighted text in a book that you want to be found, why not also bookmark the page? If you are concerned about whether a puzzle will be too difficult to solve, err on the side of simplicity. If players finish early it's a much better outcome than not solving the room at all. Considering possible player behavior when trying to solve your puzzles will give you insight into how to keep everyone moving in the right direction.

The best way to begin the design stage is to make a flowchart of your game and its puzzles. The next section goes into detail about some of the types of escape room puzzles that you can include in your game. Familiarize yourself with these as you start to organize your ideas. Whether you create a flowchart using an application such as Microsoft PowerPoint or a series of index cards or post-it notes, it will be helpful if you color-code each element of your game, including puzzles, locks, clues, and so on, that follow the same path. For example, if you have three clues that lead to the same lockbox, color-code all those items the same color. Figure 5.1 is an example of the flowchart I created using Microsoft Visio.[6]

There will be many more items in your escape room in addition to the locked boxes, so it will be helpful to create a set-up document listing all game elements, decorations, props, red herrings, clues, locks, lock boxes, and so on, along with the combinations for each of the locks. I have included a set-up template worksheet in appendix A along with a worksheet template for filling in details for each of your puzzles and challenges. You may also choose to design your entire room online using an escape room design application called Room Escape Maker (http://doctorfou.com/room-escape-maker).

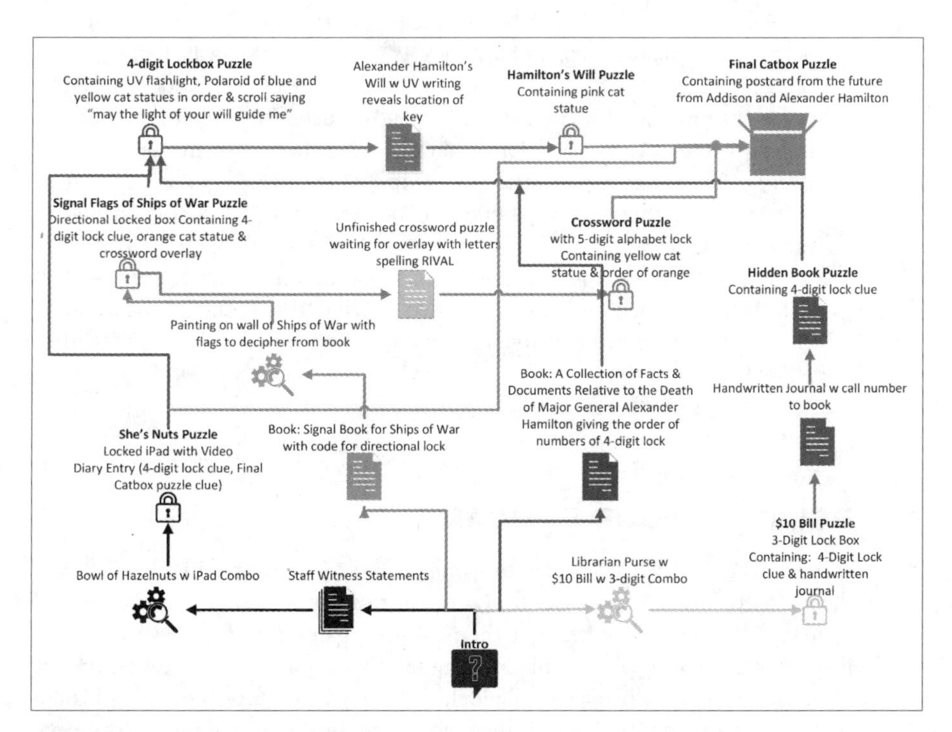

FIGURE 5.1

Flowchart of the *Alexander Hamilton Escape Room Game*

HOW TO CREATE AN ESCAPE GAME FLOWCHART

Meghin Roberts, tween and teen librarian at Flower Memorial Library (Watertown, New York), offers these helpful tips on how to create a flowchart for your own escape game.

Once you've started planning your escape room you'll quickly notice how many small components there are and that it's easy to lose track of everything. Although there are numerous ways to help you stay organized while creating your escape room, you may find a flowchart helpful.

Start at the end. What is the ultimate goal of your escape room? Put this down at the top of your page. Because everything in the escape room is leading towards this end goal, everything on your flowchart should also lead towards it. From here, build on that based on major events. Let's assume the end goal of your escape room is to have patrons unlock a box with six different locks on it and that the game ends when the item in the box is freed. The first piece of your flowchart will be "unlock box."

Below that you will have a box for each of the six locks. Color-code everything. By assigning a color to each lock, you can easily see which clues go with which specific lock. I like to be sure to put down the solution to each lock or the location of where I've hidden the key just in case something goes wrong. Next, gather every major action that needs to happen to lead to discovery of the key or combination. Any prop that must be found or clue that must be solved should be written down; for example, a lock that is opened with a four-letter word.

The last piece of the flowchart should be tools and props. List these in white, since they don't necessarily pertain to just one lock. This will help you remember all the props that you need to bring into the room and why they're relevant to the story.

DECIDING YOUR ENDGAME

What will be the final move of your game? How do you want it all to end? When designing your room, you may find it easier to start off with the endgame and then decide how players will get there. The endgame for my Alexander Hamilton room involved players placing the missing librarian's five good-luck cat statues in proper color order on a locked display box. Once they placed them in order, the magnetic lock disengaged, allowing them to discover the final locked item—a postcard sent from the future by the missing librarian and Alexander Hamilton. Throughout the game I slowly revealed both the order of the statues and the statues themselves from within various locked items, culminating in the final reveal.

Limiting the Number of Players

Once you've designed your room you will want to place a limit on the number of players who will tackle the room at one time. If your escape room consists of a series of linear puzzles in which all players must work on the same puzzle at the same time to advance, you might limit your game to a very small number of players such as one to three. If you have designed a scavenger hunt-style or larger nonlinear or mixed game involving several possible challenge paths, you can open your game to larger groups of perhaps five to ten players.

Types of Puzzle Ideas and Challenges

There is a vast array of puzzle types and challenges that can be used in escape rooms. Think about the curricular goals and/or learning outcomes that you want to achieve. How can you incorporate lessons while at the same time providing engaging puzzles? What would you like your participants to learn about: math, science, history, how to use the library catalog, how to learn to code, and so on? Think about these goals as you design your puzzles. You can use different puzzle types to test your players, teach them critical-thinking skills, team-building skills, and more. And you can also make up your own challenges to teach lessons, pass along specific skills, or simply add to the ambiance of your game.

Cyphers, Secret Codes, Message Decryption

Cyphers and secret codes are incredibly popular in escape rooms. There are many ways to incorporate these types of puzzles, but the most straightforward is to provide a group of symbols and a key to deciphering them that are placed in different areas in the room. This can be an already existing set of characters such as Morse code, braille, medieval runes, or Egyptian hieroglyphics, or your own custom set. Other ways to implement codes is to use dice with color-coded symbols on them, create anacrostic puzzles or your own alphabet, or substitute numbers for letters. My personal favorite code translation experience was in a room that had a typewriter that was designed to type out the translation to a code needed to solve the room. The Puzzled Pint code sheet (www.puzzledpint.com/files/3614/6881/3541/CodeSheet_07_2016.pdf) provides a quick reference to the most popular codes used in escape rooms. Instructables.com offers a long list of codes (www.instructables.com/id/Best-Codes/). When designing my own room, I wanted to use a code that would have been contemporary to Alexander Hamilton's time. Since Morse code

Photograph by Tuesday Moriarty.

FIGURE 5.2
Armada, by Penny Page

wasn't yet invented, I did a little research and discovered that one method of communication in the eighteenth century was via flags flown on ships of war. Each flag symbolized an action to be taken, and when flown in combination, they represented numbers that could be looked up in the code book to determine what should be done next. The code book, *Signal-Book for the Ships of War,* written by Henry Edles in 1799, is available via the University of Rhode Island's Digital Commons. I printed this out in booklet format on parchment paper to make it look old and used it as my key or legend. I have an artist in the family, so I had my mom Penny Page create a painting made with the flags I chose (see figure 5.2). These flags represent compass directions that unlock the directional lock in my escape room game.[7]

Hidden Messages

A technique that is similar to using cyphers and secret codes involves hiding messages within text. This is a great opportunity for librarians to utilize books, call numbers, and so on. One easy way to achieve this is to create a postcard decoder that is an overlay template that has key areas cut out of it.

When the decoder is placed on top of a page of text, the cutouts reveal the secret message. A complete Instructable with directions to create your own is at www.instructables.com/id/secret-postcard-decoder/.[8]

Another way to hide a message is to write or print out a jumbled message, similar to those seen on backs of cereal boxes, which can only be decoded when viewed through a red decoder lens. A red-lens viewer can be easily made or purchased, and one is included in the Breakout EDU kit. A tutorial on how to print out your own red-lens messages is found at www.madebymarzipan.com/?tutorial=diy-secret-decoder-cards.[9]

Coordinates to different books in the library's collection specifying call numbers, page numbers, and line and word numbers that make up a hidden message when combined can also be used to create and solve codes.

Light

The use of light in designing puzzles for these games is employed in over 50 percent of escape rooms worldwide, according to a survey of 175 escape room facilities. Ultraviolet ink can be used to write hidden messages text or colors that can only be seen using a black light or UV light source. Black-light puzzles are a very exciting reveal for players because they can be present in plain sight for much of the game and only revealed once the UV flashlight is provided and a clue given. I provided the clue to the lockbox holding the last remaining cat statue necessary to solve the final puzzle in my escape room game using a UV-written message on the back of Alexander Hamilton's Will, which players had access to for the entire game. They didn't know that the clue was hidden in plain sight until they unlocked a box with the UV light and clue later in the game. In this same way, glow-in-the-dark paint and pens can be used for rooms or areas that will be very dark. Light can also be used in other ways such as signaling, counting, or even for Morse code to decrypt a cypher.[10]

Hidden Objects

Placing hidden objects around the room for players to find is *the* most popular escape game puzzle type and is used in 78 percent of all rooms worldwide according to Nicholson's survey. This scavenger-hunt style puzzle is not only a fun and enjoyable activity for players, it is also an easy puzzle type that is well-suited for beginner rooms, or even for use in-between tougher puzzles in advanced rooms. I made sure to include multiple hidden objects in the Alexander Hamilton-themed room, including a hidden $10 bill with all but the first three serial numbers crossed off, which provided an early-game three-digit lock combination. I also hid a much-needed clue in a library book, and I wrote the numbers for a combination to an iPad lock screen on individual (imitation) walnuts displayed in a bowl.[11]

Object Assembly

The task of putting together mini-puzzles and/or objects is quite popular in escape room games. These objects could range from piecing together the shards of a shattered ancient vase or stitching together the paper scraps of a journal entry or paper map to assembling a jigsaw puzzle or even assembling and programming a robot to reveal a much-needed clue.[12]

Team Communication

Because escape room games are often used as team-building activities for corporate clients, it's not surprising that the second most popular puzzle type is one involving team communication. This puzzle is impossible to solve unless participants work together as a team. An example of this puzzle type might involve a team member in one room reading out the combination to a lock or a message to be typed into a computer to a team member in another room. In Escape Countdown's *Boiler Room,* one member of the players' team is kidnapped by a mysterious stranger as the rest enter the room. The players must communicate across rooms to save the abducted member and all must escape before the killer returns.[13]

Objects in Images

Used in 43 percent of escape rooms, hiding objects in images is a very popular way to provide clues. Paintings, maps, posters, and photographs can serve the dual purpose of providing both escape room décor and game functionality. A photo might depict a snapshot of your escape room with a missing vital element missing that players must search for, or alternatively contain an added item that shouldn't be there, or a misplaced object that might reveal a clue when returned to its proper place. The Ships of War painting in the Alexander Hamilton room that I designed depicts an armada with flags that provide the clue needed to unlock one of the room's main lock boxes. Another one of the boxes contains a photograph of two of the five cat statues in proper order on the final locked box.[14]

Using Something in an Unusual Way

Nearly 50 percent of escape rooms challenge players to use items in ways they normally wouldn't think of, such as using a laptop as a weight to counter-balance something. This type of out-of-the-box thinking is a key element of escape games that test players' critical-thinking skills.[15]

Noticing Something Obvious

Hiding clues in plain sight is a hallmark of escape games. Almost half of all escape rooms taunt players by placing puzzle solutions right under their noses. Numbers for a lock combination may be penciled in the margins of a journal, arrows with directions for a lock may be fixed to a decorative display, or photographs of suspects may be hung on walls.[16]

Counting

Over half of all escape rooms feature counting in their puzzles in one form or another. A basic knowledge of mathematics is necessary to solve these puzzles. One common way to achieve this type of brainteaser is to present players with an image of like objects in different colors or brands and necessitate that they add up matching items. For example, an image may feature a lineup of twenty to thirty jelly beans in pink, orange, and purple with a caption at the bottom of the image "Purple, Pink, Orange," which will prompt players to count the individually colored beans to get the combination to a three-digit lock.[17]

Riddles

Riddles are also used in many of these games. You don't have to make up your own—there are countless riddle and puzzle books available, some of which may be in your own library, such as *The Literary Pocket Puzzle Book: 120 Classic Conundrums for Book Lovers*. For my own escape room game, I used very simple riddles such as "the lawyer watches the clock" to reveal a combination number for a lock using a broken clock that is always stuck at 4 o'clock, and one that I adapted from Nicole Scherer's escape room, which was the hint "may the light of your Will guide me," to lead players to shine the UV flashlight on Alexander Hamilton's will for a clue.[18]

Locking Mechanisms

There should be a number of different types of locked objects and locking mechanisms in your escape room to add variety and interest for your players. Be sure to read the section in the description of the previous program about the Breakout EDU lock kit and the Putting Together a Lock Kit section. In addition to those ideas, you could also make your own unique locking mechanisms.

Quite popular in today's escape rooms are magnetic and electromagnetic locks that deactivate when certain triggers such as the touch of a button, the placement of objects such as statues in a specific place and/or in a specific order occur. This can be a thrilling puzzle type as it is an automatic mechanism that can unlock a drawer, a box, and so on.

An electromagnetic lock uses electricity to keep a door or drawer locked until it is opened by an electrical key of some sort that disrupts the current, at which time the magnet is deactivated. These can be unlocked remotely by touching a button, with an RFID chip, and so on. They can be built using an Arduino microcontroller board along with a power supply and RFID module. There is a very good DIY tutorial at www.makeuseof.com/tag/diy-smart-lock-arduino-rfid. The magnetic lock doesn't rely on electricity, but solely on magnetic force. It is, in essence, the same as a baby-proof magnetic lock that can be placed on cabinets to discourage children from opening unsafe drawers and doors. The magnet holds the lock in place until the matching magnet is placed on top of it to unlock it.

After seeing one of these lock types used in the *CSI: Library Murder Mystery* at the 2017 Michigan Library Association Conference, I decided to use one for my own room that would necessitate placing five Chinese good luck cat statues in a specific order for the lock to be deactivated. I used hot glue to embed the magnetic key in the bottom of just one of my statues so that when the final one was set in the proper place it would unlock my final lock box (see figure 5.3).

FIGURE 5.3
Final lockbox with Chinese good luck cat statues

Research-Based Puzzles

A puzzle type that librarians will appreciate requires players to conduct some sort of research to discern the answer to a problem. For this kind of puzzle, a reference source is provided, such as an encyclopedia, a document, or access to the Internet. This puzzle type is an excellent opportunity for librarians to incorporate bibliographic instruction in an exciting way. Perhaps conducting a Boolean search of the library's catalog could return a title containing a clue or a much-needed call number that unlocks a combination lock in the room, and so on.[19]

Sound

One of the most memorable scenes in the popular eighties film *The Goonies* was the scene in which the teens needed to play the correct notes scrawled on the back of the treasure map on the bones of a skeleton organ to unlock their way out. Why not give players a similar experience by providing a keyboard as an instructional clue? Another way to use sound is to provide clues through recorded messages, use Morse code to provide instructions, or to play a song that might contain a much-needed clue. Nicole Scherer designed an upside-down library escape room and played Diana Ross's *Upside Down* as her game soundtrack, clueing in players that they should look at the room from a different perspective.[20]

Other Puzzle Types

There are even more puzzle types than are discussed in this chapter, some of which are mentioned in chapter 3's discussion of libraries implementing escape rooms such as maze puzzles, word puzzles, crossword puzzles, Sudoku puzzles, puzzles using mirrors and reflections, and more. Your imagination is the limit.

You can make your own word puzzles using one of many free online crossword puzzle makers. As well, Teachers Pay Teachers is an excellent online resource for educational crossword, Sudoku, and other puzzles available at very low cost (https://www.teacherspayteachers.com). I purchased a great Founding Fathers crossword puzzle for my escape room for the low cost of one dollar, which was definitely worth it to save hours designing my own. If you'd rather design and make your own puzzles, here are some handy tools to get you started:

Crossword Puzzle Maker
(https://worksheets.theteacherscorner.net/make-your-own/crossword)
Jigsaw Planet
(https://www.jigsawplanet.com)

Sudoku Generator
(www.sudokuweb.org)
Cryptogram Maker
(http://puzzlemaker.discoveryeducation.comcryptogram SetupForm.asp)
Word Search Puzzle Maker
(https://www.puzzle-maker.com/wordsearch_Entry.cgi)
Discover Education Puzzle Makers
(www.discoveryeducation.com/free-puzzlemaker)
Offers word searches, math squares, mazes, number blocks, hidden message puzzles, and more.

Easter Eggs

Easter eggs are hidden bonus items in video games that don't affect the main story line but are incredibly fun to find. They could be pieces of treasure, loot, experience points, and so on. They are encountered by players who are searching for something unrelated. If there are rumors about Easter eggs in a game, players will often relentlessly search for them. Think about including real-life bonus items in your game that might thrill your players in the same way.

SETTING THE STAGE—DECORATIONS, PROPS, AND SOUNDTRACKS

Think of your escape room like a theater production. In addition to the show you're putting on, you will want to create a set filled with props, scenery, and decorations. This is a good opportunity for libraries to partner with local professional escape rooms that may be willing to provide set and prop items if you make their marketing materials available to participants. It's also an excellent occasion to work with the library's makerspace, maker club, or STEM club, which may be willing to 3-D-print props, laminate clue documents, build automated Arduino-based mechanisms for special effects, and use large-format printers to create posters, treasure maps, and so on.[21]

You may also consider incorporating actors into your escape games. You might have library staff dress up in themed costumes to greet players as they arrive, as part of the pre-game experience. You might also incorporate a character from your story line to act as a guide for players, to be a villain in your scenario, or to be a character who is rescued at the end of your game.

In addition to the visual setting of your game, you will want to have an appropriate soundtrack at the ready. This will further add to the ambiance of your game. Choose music or sound effects that are appropriate for your theme and era that will immerse your players, keeping in mind that you don't want to create a distraction. There are many free escape room soundtracks on Spotify that can be discovered by conducting a playlist search for "escape room"; on YouTube, search for "escape room soundtrack" or "escape room music." You may also search either of these resources, as well as Pandora, for appropriate music to fit your room. Tabletop Audio is an outstanding free resource that features original ten-minute music and ambiance files for use in games and stories. You can browse through categories such as sci-fi, historical, modern, nature, and so on to discover over 120 recordings. Each sound file is ten minutes long and can be combined in playlists that can be saved and set to loop infinitely so you'll have plenty of music for your escape games. Sound effects can also be found on freesound.org and both sound effects and escape room background music can be found on audiojungle.net for a price.

GAMEPLAY

The time is finally here, your room is in place, your players are ready to go, and you have the timer set. Please be sure to review the "Day of the Event" section in the description of the previous program, which includes details about the pre-game experience, gameplay, the debriefing, victory photos and props, and resetting the room.

Hints and Penalties

It is up to you to decide how players will request hints in your game and whether there will be a penalty for seeking assistance. Many one-hour games will allow players to request a total of three hints without a penalty and then each additional hint carries a penalty of a specified amount of time such as two minutes off the clock. Some games have prewritten hint cards that can be unlocked, while others have game organizers verbally relay hints to stuck players or reveal the helpful advice on computer monitors in the room. To further immerse players, some rooms have hints provided by characters within the narrative of the game.

Testing Your Room

As any newly designed game, you should rigorously test out your escape room. Start off by talking through your narrative and puzzle paths with someone else to see if they all make sense. Then arrange a beta test of your room with library staff who don't yet know about any of the puzzles you've designed. Were they able to complete the room in the allotted time? You might find that you need to expand or shorten the length of time allotted to your room. Were people standing around with nothing to do or were there too many puzzles for a small group to solve at once? In these cases, you may want to limit or expand the number of players. Talk to the beta-testers after they've gone through your room. What did they really enjoy about it? What was frustrating? Can their feedback help you provide more or better hints to make the gameplay flow more organically?

TIPS

As you are designing your first escape room, here are some tips, issues, and best practices to bear in mind.

- Create multiple copies of important clues and props that may be broken or consumed during gameplay.
- Always leave an hour between running each escape event so that you can reset all clues, locks, and props.
- Have a couple of sets of reading glasses on hand for players who may have forgotten theirs.
- Have backup batteries for flashlights.
- Test out all locks before each run of the game.
- Check all UV writing before each game to be sure it hasn't smudged/worn off.
- Limit the gameplay area so that players know what to search and where to stop if the game isn't in a dedicated room. If your scenario is a crime scene this is easily achieved by using police tape to mark the boundaries of the game.
- Create "do not touch" signs for valuable items that cannot be removed from rooms such as works of art, cabinets containing breakables/rare books, and so on.
- Set aside a table for players to collect clues, gather to brainstorm, and so on. Place important instructions here.
- Provide instructions on how to open each different type of lock.
- People are nervous when they first get in the room, so your first puzzle or two should be simple to build player confidence.
- Most people will be tired by the time the endgame comes, so make your last puzzle an easy one.
- Only use puzzle items once.
- Don't include too many red herrings to frustrate players.
- Don't assume any prior knowledge (e.g., algebra, coding, etc.) before players enter the room when designing your puzzles.
- Limit the amount of reading players must do—reading under pressure is difficult and can be frustrating.

NOTES

1. "Top 5 Types of Escape Rooms You'll Play," *Exit Strategy Games,* January 24, 2017, https://exitstrategygames.com/top-5-types-of-escape-rooms-youll-play/.
2. Ibid.
3. Ibid.
4. Ibid.
5. Adam Clare, "Tips on Designing Room Escape Games," *Reality is a Game,* July 27, 2015, www.realityisagame.com/archives/3109/tips-on-designing-room-escape-games/.
6. "Blueprint for Crafting Your First Escape Room," *Lock Paper Scissors,* https://lockpaperscissors.co/craft-1st-escape-room.
7. "55 Handpicked Escape Room Puzzles That Create Joy and Terror," *Lock Paper Scissors,* https://lockpaperscissors.co/escape-room-puzzles; "Top 11 Puzzle Ideas for Escape Rooms," *Escape Room Tips,* September 22, 2016, https://escaperoomtips.com/design/escape-room-puzzle-ideas; "History of Communication," *History World,* www.historyworld.net/wrldhis/PlainTextHistories.asp?ParagraphID=flt; Signal-Book for the Ships of War, University of Rhode Island Digital Commons, http://digitalcommons.uri.edu/cgi/viewcontent.cgi?article=1018&context=sc_pubs; Penny Page, https://www.facebook.com/Pennys-Art-377126272429356/ and http://bit.ly/2FWD2qG penelopewood12@gmail.com.
8. "100 More Great Escape Room Puzzle Ideas," *Now Escape,* January 16, 2017, http://blog.nowescape.com/100-more-great-escape-room-puzzle-ideas/.
9. Ibid.
10. S. Nicholson, "Peeking behind the Locked Door: A Survey of Escape Room Facilities," 2015, http://scottnicholson.com/pubs/erfacwhite.pdf; "Top 11 Puzzle Ideas for Escape Rooms."
11. Nicholson, "Peeking behind the Locked Door."
12. "100 More Great Escape Room Puzzle Ideas."
13. Fred Pedersen, "101 Best Escape Room Puzzle Ideas," *Now Escape,* March 18, 2016, http://blog.nowescape.com/101-best-puzzle-ideas-for-escape-rooms/.
14. Pedersen, "101 Best Escape Room Puzzle Ideas"; "55 Handpicked Escape Room Puzzles That Create Joy and Terror."
15. Pederson, "101 Best Escape Room Puzzle Ideas."
16. Ibid.
17. Pederson, "101 Best Escape Room Puzzle Ideas"; "Top 11 Puzzle Ideas for Escape Rooms."
18. Neil Somerville, *The Literary Pocket Puzzle Book: 120 Classic Conundrums for Book Lovers* (New York: Perseus), 2015; Nicole Scherer, "Do(n't) Panic: A Manual for Original Library Escape Room Events," *LibraryLady Nicole,* https://libraryladynicole.com/programs/escape-room/.
19. Pedersen, "101 Best Escape Room Puzzle Ideas."

20. Pederson, "101 Best Escape Room Puzzle Ideas"; Scherer, "Do(n't) Panic: A Manual for Original Library Escape Room Events."
21. Katie O'Reilly, "Libraries on Lockdown: Escape Rooms, a Breakout Trend in Youth Programming," *American Libraries*. September 1, 2016, https: // american librariesmagazine.org/2016/09/01/escape-rooms-libraries-on -lockdown/.

6

How to Create a Pop-Up Escape Room

NOW THAT YOU'VE MASTERED HOW TO CREATE A COMPLETE escape room from scratch, why not design a mini-game and take it with you on the road? Bring these experiences into the classroom, into retirement communities, or to library conferences and events. They can be single-day or limited-run games and can be run as a stand-alone experience or as part of a larger event. Depending on how many people you're expecting, you can design them so that they are brief games that run only thirty minutes, or even only fifteen minutes, if you'd like to accommodate a large crowd. It's up to you to determine the scope of your pop-up escape room.

POP-UP ESCAPE ROOMS

All the basic concepts of designing full-scale escape rooms remain the same for these mobile games, except that the space will vary, and the games will be shorter. You might utilize an abbreviated version of a room you've already run or designed or create something brand new for your pop-up game. Just bear in mind that your players will be under very strict time constraints, and if you'll be hosting your game at a library or other professional conference you're likely to attract many players who are new to the escape room concept.

When designing your pop-up mini-game, remember that it is meant to be a short experience. Therefore, you will want to limit your paths to major puzzles down to one or make it even simpler by just having a handful of mini puzzles for players to solve. Your players will likely not be escape game connoisseurs, so you don't want to challenge them so much that they don't win.

Design your props and lockables so that they are easily transported or shipped to the destination space. This will limit your choices of items like furniture and bookshelves, so you'll have to come up with creative ways to set your stage and establish your setting. Some easy ways to do this include bringing your own background music and making sure to have plenty of theme-specific props. Don't forget about incorporating backdrops, which can add to the atmosphere and even be used as some of your puzzles.

If you are organizing a major event or professional conference at which you'd like to include an escape room, another way to go is to partner with a local commercial escape room. They will likely be enthusiastic about designing a pop-up escape room to run as a part of your event because it will spread the word about their business.

DESIGNING PORTABLE ESCAPE ROOMS

These tips and words of advice have been contributed by Emma Rochon of Improbable Escapes in Kingston, Ontario, an expert in designing mobile escape experiences. As of 2018, her team has presented internationally on the topic and created over twenty-five unique experiences in historic towers, houses, hotels, parks, forts, and schools. They have also taught hundreds of people how simple, cost-efficient, and fun it is to create and run portable escape rooms.

Portable escape experiences are an unstoppable phenomenon sweeping the escape room industry. They are a cost-effective way for escape room companies to increase profit while increasing their reach and market. It's a method for educational facilities to gamify various topics, or to add value to different topics for museums, libraries, or conventions.

The language around portable games vary depending on where you go, but there are a few general terms you should know:

Mobile escape rooms are in trailers or other vehicles that are *driven from one location to another.*

Transportable escape rooms are in tents, inflatable frames, or pods that can be easily fully set up and taken down. *They are designed to move often and easily.*

Pop-up escape games are installations that can go into brick and mortar locations such as libraries, towers, historic properties. They are themed around that space and can be experienced for days or months. The beautiful thing about transportable games is that simplicity is key. When creating your own pop-up game, you can create a fun and popular game by prioritizing four things: difficulty level, theme, safety, and creativity.

Here are some design principles to get you started:

Difficulty Level

It's okay if it's easy! Brick and mortar escape rooms can get away with low escape rates but pop-up games running between 5 and 30 minutes should have an escape rate of 80 to 100 percent. The experience needs to be worth the time investment. If the team is frustrated and not solving anything the entire time, they likely won't have fun or want to play again. Ideally, you want a series of small successes leading to the final escape.

Hints are okay and expected. There's an art to delivering clues that push teams in the right direction, while still letting them solve the challenges themselves. Establish the number of hints before the game begins. Never tell teams the answer, but tell the team where to focus. This is often enough for them to solve it themselves! Become more specific if they ask for more clarification.

Adjust! Adjust! Adjust! If you're running the game more than once, beta testing is necessary. It's easy to get attached to puzzles when you've put a lot of time and energy into them, but remember things that may seem easy and logical to you can be difficult for others. You need to recognize weak points and be able to improve areas with problems.

Theme

Stay consistent. Design puzzles around the theme and location. Say you're making a transportable 10-minute jail cell experience. You can create clues from many things in the room such as the bed, sink, toilet, or bars. A pirate ship wheel, parrot, and eyepatch wouldn't make sense within a jail cell theme. For example, you could fish a key out of the sink or toilet with a magnet to open a box that has extra sheets for the bed. The blankets have holes in them, which overlay on the mattress in the cell to reveal a code. This consistency will allow teams to stay fully immersed in the experience.

Safety

It is better to be safe than sorry; safety should always be the top priority. Everything that you design should be completely foolproof. Make sure to remove all tripping hazards, provide enough light, remove all sharp objects, and keep electric wires hidden away. You're not doing this for the average customer; you're creating a safe experience for the customer that's one in a hundred, who has a sense of reckless abandon for their safety and will injure themselves because they're not paying attention.

Stay on the ground! Unless you are entirely sure no one will ever fall, design everything in a pop-up so customers keep at least one foot on the floor at all times.

Creativity

Be unique! The most important thing to remember is that teams are signing up because they want to have fun. The more creative, surprising, and unusual you can be, the better. Have fun with the design and teams will have fun playing!

••••••••

POP-UP BREAKOUT GAMES

Most escape games, or breakout experiences involve breaking out of a room or space, but what about breaking in? How about just having a locked box at your table in the exhibit hall at a conference that passersby can try to break in to? The Michigan Library Association Annual Conference hosted one of these games during their 2017 event and it really spiced up the opening night reception. (Organizers are shown in figure 6.1) Attendees were split up into groups of four and assigned a team name. They were given a list of vendors to visit in the exhibit hall to ask for an envelope with their team name on it. Each of the envelopes collected had a clue or a puzzle inside that the team needed to solve together. Most of these were word, cipher, and trivia puzzles that once solved led to cracking the final puzzle. The locked box at the table had a hasp with several locks on it that could be opened once the team had unraveled all the brainteasers posed by organizers. Once opened, the box was filled with handfuls of candy (a welcomed sight for conference-goers!) that could be shared by all participants.

FIGURE 6.1
Organizers of the Michigan Library Association Breakout Game: Kathleen Zaenger, Janice Heilman, Brandi Tambasco, and Scott Drapalik of the Howell Carnegie District Library

HOST A POP-UP BREAKOUT EVENT ESCAPE GAME

This outstanding pop-up-style escape game was contributed by Janice Heilman, Youth Services Librarian, and Brandi Tambasco, Adult Services Librarian, of the Howell Carnegie District Library in Howell, MI.

A pop-up escape game, also called a "breakout" is a fantastic way to engage attendees at an event or conference, not just with each other but also with your exhibitors. The goal of this kind of event is not only to entertain participants by providing an outlet to interact with each other, but also to drive traffic to your vendors in the exhibit hall. We organized just such an activity for all conference goers during the opening reception of the Michigan Library Association annual conference in 2017, and we can tell you how to run one for your own library or association.

Most breakouts are designed for a small group of players; however, this type of event needs to scale much larger. We estimated about 160 participants for our game during our annual association conference's opening reception. We suggest that you limit your teams to between two and four players each since you'll be organizing walk-ups of conference-goers who may be together or solos. With such a large scope, strive to keep it as simple as you can. This type of game should take no more than 15 minutes for a team to complete and not be *too* challenging for conference attendees at the end of long days. To create a game for your teams to visit as many vendors as reasonably possible, you'll want to start planning well before the actual event.

Planning and Preparation

Dedicate library staff to the planning and preparation stages of the game. We had nine staffers involved in this process. Begin several months before the event. Here are the steps to take to create such a large-scale game.

Create a Story Line

The simplest way to start planning your game is to borrow and adapt a simple story and theme from an existing, free Breakout EDU game. We used the one called "M&M Mastermind," about outsmarting a Mastermind to access their locked M&M stash, available from https://platform.BreakoutEDU.com/game/mmmastermind.

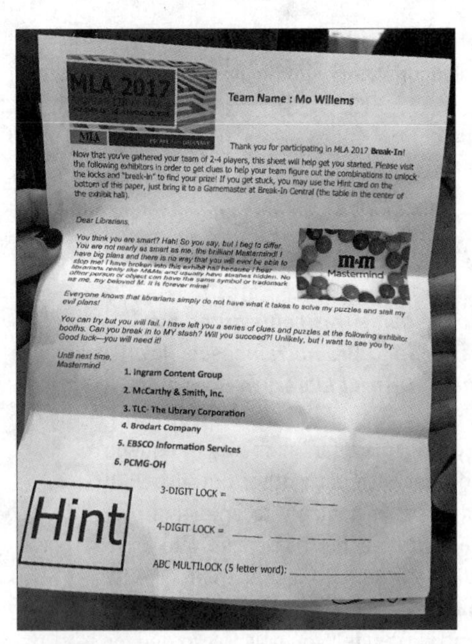

MLA 2017

MLA

Team Name : Mo Willems

Thank you for participating in MLA 2017 **Break-In!**

Now that you've gathered your team of 2-4 players, this sheet will help get you started. Please visit the following exhibitors in order to get clues to help your team figure out the combinations to unlock the locks and "break-in" to find your prize! If you get stuck, you may use the Hint card on the bottom of this paper, just bring it to a Gamemaster at Break-In Central (the table in the center of the exhibit hall).

Dear Librarians,

You think you are smart? Hah! So you say, but I beg to differ. You are not nearly as smart as me, the brilliant Mastermind! I have big plans and there is no way that you will ever be able to stop me! I have broken into this exhibit hall because I hear librarians really like M&Ms and usually have stashes hidden. No other person or object can have the same symbol or trademark as me, my beloved M. It is forever mine!

m&m Mastermind

Everyone knows that librarians simply do not have what it takes to solve my puzzles and stall my evil plans!

You can try but you will fail. I have left you a series of clues and puzzles at the following exhibitor booths. Can you break in to MY stash? Will you succeed?! Unlikely, but I want to see you try. Good luck—you will need it!

Until next time,
Mastermind

1. Ingram Content Group
2. McCarthy & Smith, Inc.
3. TLC- The Library Corporation
4. Brodart Company
5. EBSCO Information Services
6. PCMG-OH

Hint

3-DIGIT LOCK = ___ ___ ___

4-DIGIT LOCK = ___ ___ ___ ___

ABC MULTILOCK (5 letter word): ______________

FIGURE 6.2
Letter from the Mastermind

We printed this game's adapted story—a letter from the Mastermind (see figure 6.2) to the participants—on the instruction sheet handed out to each team at the start of their game run. We also used the same three-digit and ABC lock codes as the Breakout EDU game.

You may choose to follow our lead, choose and adapt another such game that fits the theme of your event, or make up your own. When choosing a game to modify, make sure you have all the required locks used in the game. If you choose to create your own new game from scratch, be sure to factor extra time for this into your overall time line for your event.

Create Groups of Exhibitors and Paths for Each Team

Design paths for teams to follow to receive their game clues. There is a two-fold reason for this. It will help you avoid bottlenecks during your event and best utilize the whole exhibit hall space. It will also ensure each exhibitor is visited at least once, keeping things as fair as possible for vendors and satisfying the goal to have attendees visit as many exhibitors as reasonably possible. For this, you need to do a little math.

First, determine your numbers. How many teams do you estimate will play your game? How many vendors will your exhibit hall feature? How many clues will your game have? These are the important numbers you need to proceed with planning your event. Find the common denominator between your maximum team number and total number of vendors to help you determine how many clues you need. Don't fear the math!

As mentioned above, we estimated 160 participants total for our event. With teams of two to four players each, we needed to plan for up to eighty teams (if teams were composed of only two players; less than that if they were made up of three to four, but you should plan for the maximum to avoid nasty surprises). The total number of exhibitors we had was sixty. With those two nice round numbers, we had a lovely common denominator of ten.

Using this lovely number, we divided the list of sixty vendors into groups of six, so that for every ten teams that participated, each exhibitor was visited at least once, with a maximum of eight teams visiting each vendor. This meant each team would visit six different vendors and, voila, that's how many clues we needed: our magic number six! This number worked out well for our event and we wouldn't recommend making players visit many more than six exhibitors after a long day at the conference.

Now comes the tricky part. To avoid traffic-flow issues, we shifted each team's starting exhibitor so their order was different. We decided each team would visit a list of six exhibitors *in a specific order* to receive each one of their clues. This took effort to plan and prepare, with one staff member figuring out the paths based on the exhibit hall map and several other staffers sorting, organizing, and labeling the clues in their proper number and team order and banding them together into a packet for each exhibitor. Sounds like a lot of work, but it can be done!

Though we felt it necessary to take these extra steps to manage traffic flow and require teams to acquire their clues in a specific order, you may find this added effort to stagger the teams' start locations unnecessary, especially if you want to keep your efforts simple. Eliminating that part of the planning and preparation would certainly make this stage easier and streamline the organization of your game.

Create Clues

Now that you have your story line and know how many clues your game needs, create those clues to lead the players to the correct lock codes. Use your magic number of clues, in our case six, to decide how many hints each clue would give for the lock codes. We decided that each clue would generally provide two hints for each of the three locks.

Most breakout games incorporate technology into their clues, for example, accessing a website to find new information and solve puzzles. However, to prevent any technology mishaps, especially because we were running our event outside our home turf and could not comfortably depend on the reliability of the available conference Wi-Fi connection (who hasn't had trouble at a convention getting a signal with their smart device?), we kept it old school and used only paper-based clues; these also conveniently fit into envelopes for easy distribution. We recommend using only paper clues for your event, too. However, if you feel confident enough in your or your team's technology troubleshooting skills, by all means incorporate some cool tech clues into your game.

Whether you use our clues, adapt ones from a different game, or create your own, be sure to label your final clue as the last clue so that participants know they have everything they need to solve the game. Include a final reminder about where to go (your game's headquarters) and what to do (talk with a gamemaster) once they think they have solved the game and figured all the lock codes.

To duplicate our game, here are the specific clues we created and the order in which the teams received them. You can also access our clue files in a shared Google Drive folder at https://goo.gl/irGBqt.

For our first clue, we used a trick we learned from a different breakout we ran at our library (Dr. Johnson's Lab Zombie Apocalypse breakout, found at https://platform.BreakoutEDU.com/game/dr-johnsons-lab). We placed a stack of three different colors of small sticky notes in an envelope; the different quantities of each color gave the players the three-digit code solution. For example, for a three-digit lock code of 413, our clue envelope had a small stack with four yellow sticky notes on top, one green sticky note in the middle, and three violet sticky notes on the bottom.

Our second clue was trivia about the M&M candy's history, which contained the four-digit lock code as well as the order of the three-digit code's numbers from the first clue. For this clue, we used trivia about "What the 'M's Stand for in M&Ms" and some "Bonus Facts" about the candy, available online at www.todayifoundout.com/index.php/2010/05/what-the-ms-stand-for-in-mms. The first sentence of the trivia contains the four-digit lock code, the year 1941. The sentence about the order of the original M&M colors provides players with the order of the three-digit lock sticky note clue (yellow, green, and violet).

For the third clue, players solved a word scramble of five different location names with the aid of a map printed at the bottom of the clue's sheet. Once unscrambled, two of the answers are five letters long, qualifying as the code for the ABC lock, with one as a red herring to make the game a bit more challenging without making it too difficult. The clue sheet listed the scrambled words in the order to be unscrambled with blanks next to them for players to fill them in. The place names we used were Lansing (the location of our conference), Nashville, Bronx, Boise, and Phoenix, with Boise as the correct five-digit ABC lock code. We created the map by using Google Maps and taking a screenshot of the completed map.

The fourth clue was an image of a fake boarding pass with its airport code highlighted for a flight to Boise, which was one of the locations from the third clue's word scramble results. This helps eliminate the red herring in the previous clue. You can find the image we used in the Google Drive folder link above.

The fifth clue was a ransom note that refers to the four-digit number 1941, found in our second clue. You can use the one we made from our Google Drive folder or make up your own ransom note using the website www.ransomizer.com.

Finally, our sixth and final clue was an image of a fake driver's license for the Mastermind (tying the clue back to the story), which had the three-digit and four-digit codes hidden within the listed address and date of birth. We also labeled this clue sheet as the last clue and included a final reminder of what to do and where to go when the game was finished. This last clue can also be found in the Google Drive folder linked above.

Create Team Names

Come up with names for each of your maximum number possible of teams. The team name generation may be the quickest part of your planning and prep, as well as an excellent opportunity to be creative and/or play up your theme. In this step, we blatantly appealed to our audience's sensibilities. Librarians *love* anything book related, so we decided each team would be named after a famous author. We simply sat down and began typing a list of eighty authors into an Excel spreadsheet and then sorted it alphabetically. Easy peasy!

Assemble All Clues and Label for Each Team

Once you have all your clues and the team names set, make as many copies of each of your clues as your maximum team total plus a few extras. Organize these into discreet packets or containers (e.g., envelopes), and clearly label them with the team name and clue number so you know what is in each.

Because we had only paper clues, with five of our clues being simply sheets of letter-sized paper and the other clue just a small stack of small sticky notes, they all fit well into a standard-size mailing envelope.

This all sounds simple enough, but counting out sticky notes and making sure the right clues go into the right envelopes takes quite a bit of time for a game of this size, especially because the order of the clues mattered. This step was one of the most time-consuming, so plan ahead!

Sort All Clues by Which Exhibitor Is to Distribute Them

Once you've got all your clues in their proper envelopes, you'll want to sort them into piles for each exhibitor based on the paths you determined earlier. Each exhibitor will receive a packet of envelopes with the name of the team to whom that vendor should give the clue written or labeled on the front, bound together with a rubber band.

Place a sticky note on each packet listing the name of the designated vendor, so you know to whom it should be given when the packets are distributed prior to the event's start. This was also a very time-consuming step.

Create an Instruction Sheet for Participating Teams

Rather than shouting gameplay rules over the din of a busy exhibit hall, prepare an instruction sheet to give to each participating team. This sheet should list the team's name, basic instructions for the breakout, the game's story line (in our case, the M&M Mastermind's letter), the list of exhibitors to visit to receive their clues, and what types of locks need to be solved (for our game, a three-digit lock, a four-digit lock, and a five-letter ABC lock) with space to write in solutions. The only two items on this sheet that will vary by team is the team name and the list of exhibitors to visit.

The instruction sheet should also let the teams know where to go if they need a hint or have any other questions about the game. You will need a booth or table from which to run the game. Come up with a name for your game's headquarters (ours was simply Breakout Central) and list that and its location on the instruction sheet. Our Breakout Central was centrally located in the middle of the exhibit hall.

In the end, we had eighty instruction sheets, each bearing one of the team names we generated previously. We kept and handed out the sheets in alphabetical order, because our paths were ordered that way; for every ten instruction sheets we handed out, each exhibitor was visited by at least one team. This helped us easily track both the number of participating teams and the number of exhibitors visited for post-game statistics while also ensuring a fair distribution of visits to exhibitors. A copy of our team instruction sheet can be found in the Guides folder on the shared Google Drive (https://drive.google.com/drive/folders/1xeW8vCRS_ZKIPlixDEP8TibCiqGJIMV7).

Borrow Additional Breakout EDU Boxes and Accessories from Other Libraries

To avoid participants having to wait in a long line to test their lock code solutions, you may want to borrow Breakout EDU boxes, hasps, and locks from other libraries in your region. We had a total of five boxes for our event, which worked out great for our game. Make careful note of the lock codes used for each lock and include this with each box when you return them to their owning libraries—the librarians there will thank you!

Set All Locks to Game Code Solutions, Fill Boxes with Prizes, and Close with Hasps and Locks

Make a list of all the locks and their codes. Use this list to prepare all the Breakout EDU boxes you'll use in your game. Double check to make sure you've filled your boxes with prizes before you set the hasps and lock the boxes. Although it is always good to have a pair of bolt cutters with you when running a breakout game, giving yourself plenty of time to prepare the boxes in a quiet, distraction-free area helps prevent any errors in setting your lock codes.

We used three locks in our game: a three-digit lock, a four-digit lock, and an ABC lock with a five-letter word as the code (these locks are standard in the Breakout EDU kit). Because we used five total boxes, we had to set five different locks of each kind to the same code. The day before the event, we set aside an hour to organize the locks and prepare the boxes, making careful note of which code unlocked which lock. We made sure to have our trusty bolt cutters on hand just in case.

Keeping with our breakout's story theme, we filled each Breakout EDU box with a variety of mini bags of M&Ms as small rewards for each participant. Though we only used one kind of candy as a reward, the participants were pleased with the variety of M&Ms (regular, peanut, and caramel). The event took place a couple of weeks before Halloween, so bulk, fun-size candy was plentiful. If you are not so fortunate with the timing of your event, plan your purchase in advance. Fill your boxes with any rewards that fit your event's theme.

Set up each Breakout EDU box you use in your game the same way with the same locks, lock codes, and prizes inside, so when each team returns with their code solutions, they can try to unlock any one of your prepared boxes.

Create a Gamemaster Guide

Depending on the size of your event, you will likely need several staffers administering your breakout game at the event; we had seven volunteers from our library and the conference planning committee to help facilitate our game. These intrepid volunteers will be your gamemasters (GMs) who will be expected to know the lock code solutions and to provide hints as needed to teams who are stuck or just having a little trouble making it to the next step. The GMs will be stationed at your game's headquarters in the exhibit hall to assist with unlocking the boxes when teams are ready, and to relock the boxes once teams have unlocked them and claimed their prize.

Compile a detailed guide for all GMs to introduce them to your breakout game, explain the game's flow, and detail their responsibilities as facilitators. The guide should include the instruction sheet each team will receive and a copy of each clue, with notes on how and which locks the facilitators help to solve. A copy of our gamemaster guide can be found in the Guides folder on the shared Google Drive.

Create Exhibitor Guide

To alleviate any sense of burden or pressure and make their participation as simple and easy as possible, put together a brief guide for vendors explaining the game and their roles in it. The guide should outline the game's flow and what they should expect during the event. Here you can also thank the vendors for their participation and ask them to direct teams with any questions to the gamemasters at your game's headquarters. Distribute a copy of the guide to all exhibitors along with their clue packets prior to the game's start. A copy of our exhibitor guide can be found the Guides folder on the Google Drive.

Have Extras!

Keep several additional copies of each part of the game at your booth including the team instruction sheet, the gamemaster guide, the exhibitor guide, and each clue. Keep them all together, set aside from the main game supplies and label them as extras. This can come in handy if a team loses one of its clues during the short game run and needs another one to finish the game, as happened during our event.

Because our clues were mostly simple sheets of paper, we simply stapled them all together into a nice, easily-referenced packet with the number and color of the sticky notes that made up our first clue written on the front.

Day-Before and Day-Of Preparation

The day before the event is the perfect time to prepare all the Breakout EDU boxes. Find a quiet, distraction-free location to assemble the boxes—a helper familiar with the game (a gamemaster or, as in our case, a fellow game designer and event organizer) will make the task go more quickly. Set aside at least one hour for this task; it should take less time than that, but you do not want to feel rushed and make mistakes. Bolt cutters are great, but you don't want to have to use them!

On the day of the event, visit all exhibitors to distribute their clue envelopes and guides well before the game starts. Use a cart or hand truck to make your deliveries, because you may have a few boxes full of many clue envelopes. We used a foldable wheeled crate with a long handle to scoot around the exhibit hall during the vendors' designated set-up time to distribute our exhibitor guides and clues and explain the game.

Before your event's start time, set up your game headquarters booth on tables in the exhibit hall, and clearly mark it. Greet your gamemaster volunteers and staff, go over the guide to the game, and answer any questions they have.

Gameplay

Have a greeter at the door to the exhibit hall to talk up your game to attendees and direct interested conference-goers to your game's headquarters. When players arrive at your booth, don't stress about putting people into teams. We found that team generation happened naturally as interested players approached the booth. If needed, you can help form teams of people who are solos at the conference as well as organize groups of colleagues.

When the teams are ready to start, have your gamemasters briefly explain the game, hand out the instruction sheets, and direct each team to return to your headquarters if they

- have any questions about the game (rather than ask exhibitors)
- need any help during the game
- are ready to try their deciphered codes to unlock the box

Plenty of people will never have heard of a "breakout," so your gamemasters should also be prepared to explain the concept: a breakout game is a kind of portable escape room experience with puzzles to solve to help break *into* a box, rather than *out of* a room.

During the game, if the participants use the wrong code, feel free to give as many hints as needed to help them find the right answer. You want to ensure everyone enjoys the breakout and not become frustrated by getting stuck on a clue.

After each team completes the game, unlocks one of the boxes, and receives their reward, be sure to snap a photo (see figure 6.3) with your

FIGURE 6.3
My team and me holding up our victory signs after we "broke out"

smartphones of all the team members holding one of the many pre-printed and laminated Breakout EDU completion signs (these can be found on BreakoutEDU.com). We chose not to bring any negative signs ("we almost broke out," etc.) so as not to dampen anyone's enjoyment.

With a little encouragement, all our players were happy to choose their own signs. Have them spread out on a table or other surface to make selection easy. Encourage your participants to be as enthusiastic and whacky as they want in the photos; their spirits will be running high after their joint accomplishment of winning the game, so you'll want to capitalize on this and capture it. Shortly after the event you can post all your great completion photos to the conference or association's social media sites. Let the participants know where they can go online to see their photos.

In our game, every team who played won by unlocking all the locks on the Breakout EDU boxes and claiming an M&M candy prize from within. All of our participants said they had a great time playing our game and would try another breakout/escape experience in the future. Our large-scale breakout event was very successful; we hope yours is, too!

•••••••

7

How to Create an Escape Room Enthusiasts Club

A FANTASTIC WAY TO PROMOTE CRITICAL THINKING AND CREativity in the library and pass along STEAM (science, technology, engineering, arts, and mathematics) skills is to create an escape room enthusiasts club. This type of program has the potential to engage patrons with many different interest areas and backgrounds. Escape rooms appeal to gamers, because of their challenging puzzles; makers, because of the ways they use unique mechanisms for props and locks; techies and coders because of how they integrate technology; and artists because of the immersive design and storytelling aspects. This diverse program would simultaneously promote a culture of making in the library, a resource for designing future programming in the form of escape game events, and an inspiration for patrons to work together to create something of their own.

If your library has other clubs like gaming, anime, and book clubs, you can look to them for guidance and structure, as well as for potential members and future partnerships. Here are some recommendations for how to create an escape room enthusiasts club in your library.

AUDIENCE

You will want to specify an age range for your club. Determine the minimum and maximum ages and include them on all promotional materials: your Facebook page, flyers, announcements in your newsletter, website, and so on. An example of this might be "open to library patrons ages eight through eighteen." Escape rooms are very popular with all age ranges, so you'll need to decide which ages are appropriate for your library. This type of club would be popular with both kids and teens. Because it would offer activities to help prepare them for college and the job market, you may want to consider including both demographics.

LOGISTICS

Where will you meet in the library? Because many of the activities that this club will be taking on will involve brainstorming with and learning from fellow members, it will be noisy. You will need to find an area of the library where this type of enterprise will not disturb others who are studying or quietly reading. But keep in mind that many of the activities will involve making and using maker equipment such as 3-D printers, so you will definitely want to partner with your library's makerspace, especially when deciding on the times and days the club will meet. This will likely be an after-school club, so think about when your kids will be able to come to the library. Check in with interested members to see if meeting on weekdays or weekends will work best for them. And finally, decide how often your club will meet. Keep in mind that most club programs meet once per month.

COMMUNICATION AND MARKETING

Communication is key for any successful venture, and an escape room enthusiasts club is no different. You will need to make sure that all your current and potential members know about the exciting programming that you have planned. A great way to do this is to have that information available through multiple outlets so that if kids don't see it coming through one way, they may notice it another. A Facebook group is a great start. These are free and easy to set up and are a quick way to promote your club with photos, videos, and flyers. Your members will not only be informed about upcoming events and meetings, but your marketing efforts will attract new members. It's also a way to have patrons RSVP to events such as escape room field trips, presentations by guest speakers, workshops, and brainstorming sessions.

Instagram is an excellent social media tool for promotion and marketing. It's a place for you to upload not only photos of your clubs, including escape room games and events, but also from maker sessions, brainstorming meetings, and more. This will demonstrate to potential members that this is an interesting and engaging club that they might want to join.

Consider setting up an e-mail list for members to let them know about possible cancellations, send them reminders about upcoming meetings and events, and send out e-mail blasts about important news.

Although it may seem like an analog marketing technique, designing flyers to post around the library or put out on tables for people to pick up is still an effective form of promotion. Flyers designed digitally can also be posted to social media outlets such as Instagram and Facebook.

And finally, be sure that there is a place on your library's website for your club. Both members and parents will look there for information about it.

STAFFING

You will probably only need one or two staff members to helm this type of club, especially if you are partnering with your library's makerspace for the maker activities. While planning the programming at the beginning of the club may be a bit time intensive, once the membership grows and the kids become comfortable, they will assume the lead when it comes to determining the direction of the club and its activities.

PLAN THE PROGRAM

What will kids and teens do as a part of your escape room enthusiasts club? The possibilities are endless, but you may want to have some starter activities planned for the first few meetings to get things going. Don't be afraid to be fluid with your planning: as with most activities that involve making, your initial direction may lead to alternate endeavors. What might start out as a simple prop-building session may lead to a multi-week project that involves programming said prop using a Raspberry Pi or Arduino board to respond to player interaction. Some activities that members might take on during club meetings include:

- Planning and designing their own escape rooms
- Brainstorming puzzle ideas
- Building props
- 3-D printing and making props in makerspaces
- Partnering with and visiting local escape rooms
- Inviting escape room designers to come to meetings as guest speakers to inspire and give advice
- Presenting craft, art, writing, and technology workshops
- Hosting Hour of Code events

PLANNING AN ESCAPE ROOM EVENT

Once your escape room enthusiasts club gains some momentum, you might suggest that kids and teens work together to create their own escape room, which would include creating puzzles, planning a theme, writing the narrative, designing the room from an aesthetic perspective, and running the event. Librarians at the Morton-James Public Library organized a program in which a group of forty children created a zombie-themed escape room over the course of several weeks. To do this you will need to organize a schedule of meetings during which you will work on specific elements of the game; for example, one meeting might be dedicated to brainstorming a theme for the room while another might be devoted to puzzle design. Remember that in the beginning, smaller is better. You might limit the club's first escape game to a 20-minute room and the puzzles to one major path or just a series of smaller challenges. The kids will learn from the issues and triumphs of their initial room as they move on to designing larger games.[1]

STEAM ACTIVITIES

There are many opportunities for developing STEAM skills in this type of program. Here are just a few ideas.

Creating and Solving Puzzles: So many different puzzle types appear in escape room games, as you read in a previous chapter on how to create your escape room from scratch. Entire meeting sessions can be used to try out and explore these varying puzzle types, and to create challenges for their peers. Everything from Sudoku and word puzzles to cyphers and riddles can be undertaken.

Making Props and Programming Technology: Props, locking mechanisms, and the technology that adds automation to these games open up a world of possibilities.

- Kids can learn to 3-D design props using 3-D modeling software such as Tinkercad and see their designs become reality (see figure 7.1).
- Magnetic and electromagnetic locks are often used in escape games to add a bit of magic to the experience. Kids can learn how they work and build their own.
- Motion sensors that react when players carry out certain movements can be created using Microsoft Kinect technology or Arduino boards.
- Touch boards can be used to create seemingly magical results by playing sounds or music when players place items in certain areas or touch certain objects.

FIGURE 7.1
Chinese good luck cat statues 3-D printed and painted for my escape room

- Robots can be built and programmed to react to player input for puzzles and mazes.
- Kids can build cryptex boxes like those in *The Da Vinci Code* to hide secret messages.

Exploring the Arts: Rich artwork, an engaging narrative, and a fitting soundtrack all work to make an escape room experience much more immersive. These areas also open plenty of opportunities for learning in the library.

- Kids can learn how to program music and sound effects using a Raspberry Pi and the Sonic Pi software application.
- Club members can learn how to come up with story ideas, storyboard them, create outlines, develop a cohesive narrative, and write content for the game.
- Artistic members can develop scenery and backdrops for the game, including paintings that can hold clues, decorative pieces and props for the room, and even flyers and posters for the escape room event.

CONNECT WITH THE COLLECTION

Don't forget to plug the library and its resources at every opportunity. Does your collection feature titles on Raspberry Pi and Arduino boards? What about 3-D printing or books on how to write effectively? You might bring some of these titles to the club meetings to make it easier for patrons to borrow them.

FUNDRAISING

Some of the activities in this club will involve costs. You could pass those expenses along to your patrons and have them purchase their own supplies, or you could come up with the funds from the library's budget. But just in case you don't have the funds at the ready, there are many ways you can come up with them. Here are a few suggestions (refer also to chapter 2 for additional information)[2]:

- Investigate your state library's resources.
- Start a campaign on Donors Choose (https://www.donorschoose.org) or Indiegogo (https://www.indiegogo.com and crowdfund your club).
- Ask your community to donate resources and supplies.
- Research programs like
  - IMLS (Institute of Museum and Library Services) grants (https://www.imls.gov/grants/apply-grant/available-grants)
  - Lowe's Toolbox for Education (http://toolboxforeducation.com)
  - Cognizant's Making the Future Grant (https://www.cognizant.com/company-overview/sustainability/educational-opportunity)
  - YALSA Awards, Grants, Stipends and Scholarships (www.ala.org/yalsa/awardsandgrants/yalsaawardsgrants)
  - YALSA Funding, Awards, and Grants (http://wikis.ala.org/yalsa/index.php/Funding,_Awards_and_Grants)
  - YALSA Teen Tech Week Grants (http://teentechweek.ning.com/page/grants-funding)
  - Botball Robotics sponsorships (www.botball.org/scholarships)
  - Rockwell Collins Charitable Corporation Grants (https://www.rockwellcollins.com/Our_Company/Corporate_Responsibility/Community_Overview/Charitable_Giving.aspx)
  - W. K. Kellogg Foundation Grants (https://www.wkkf.org)

RESOURCES

YALSA's Maker and DIY Projects Resources
(http://wikis.ala.org/yalsa/index.php/Maker_ percent26_DIY_Programs)

YALSA's Making in the Library Toolkit
(www.ala.org/yalsa/sites/ala.org.yalsa/files/content/YALSA percent20Making percent20Toolkit.pdf)

Instructables
(www.instructables.com/)

Make it @ Your Library
(http://makeitatyourlibrary.org)

Code Club World
(https://www.codeclubworld.org/1)

NOTES

1. Jennifer Thoegersen and Rasmus Thoegersen, "Pure Escapism: Programs That Pop," *Library Journal,* July 18, 2016, https://lj.libraryjournal.com/2016/07/opinion/programs-that-pop/pure-escapism-progams-that-pop.
2. Jessica Snow, "Looking to Create a Makerspace in Your Library? Here Are Some Ideas," *YALSA Blog,* October 14, 2015, http://yalsa.ala.org/blog/2015/10/14/looking-to-create-a-makerspace-in-your-library-here-are-some-ideas/; Library Grants, Scholastic, www.scholastic.com/librarians/programs/grants.htm.

8

How to Host an Immersive Experience

IMMERSIVE EXPERIENCES SUCH AS THOSE DISCUSSED IN CHAPTER 1 intrigue and engross participants and are sure to draw many curious patrons to your events. They may even attract people who don't normally visit the library. There are many possibilities for creating these types of events for your library. Here are a few ideas to get you started.

DETERMINE THE OUTCOME

First create a plan to determine your target outcomes for the event or experience that you're planning. What do you want participants to learn about the library or the special exhibit that you're hosting? Is there an educational objective or is this an outreach event designed to foster a positive experience within the library? Establishing a list of target objectives or learning outcomes will guide you as you form a list of activities and challenges for your participants.

PICK A THEME

To make your experience as immersive as it can possibly be, it is important to focus on a singular theme. This can be a literary theme for book-centered events, a movie or television-show theme, a video-game theme, or a genre theme (e.g., sci-fi). Ask your patrons if they have preferences when it comes to themed events and exhibits. Perhaps you have a large anime constituency at the library, or fans of television shows like *Star Trek* or *Game of Thrones*. Some possibilities for themes include:

- Popular book and movie series such as *The Maze Runner, Divergent,* or *The Hunger Games*
- Marvel or DC comic books and movies
- Disney movies
- Fandoms such as *Dr. Who, Harry Potter, Lord of the Rings, Star Wars,* and *Supernatural*

CREATE AMBIANCE

You can easily create ambiance and a sense of place through decorations, an appropriate music soundtrack, and themed refreshments such as Butterbeer for *Harry Potter* events, tacos for a *Deadpool* event, or candy sushi for anime-themed events. You may also consider providing an element of cosplay for participants by offering visitors the chance to wear class robes and ties for *Harry Potter* events, scarves for *Dr. Who* events, or red shirts or Vulcan ears for *Star Trek* events, and so on.

Each year, the Salt Lake County Library hosts an incredibly popular Harry Potter Yule Ball, which has drawn 1,500 costumed attendees over its three years. This immersive event, organized by senior teen services librarian Carrie Rogers-Whitehead, includes a Platform 9¾ photo booth, a Diagon Alley, a McGonagall's Game Room that features board games, a Divination Room with fortune telling, crafts like wand making, and activities such as dancing and a House Cup competition. Special guests have included the Rocky Mountain Muggles costume troupe, Marshmallow the barn owl, and the organization Creature Encounters, which has brought along live tarantulas and pythons.[1]

ESTABLISH A MISSION

Why not offer participants a mission to go along with your event? Get them excited about coming in and taking part in a scenario. It doesn't have to be as extravagant or complex as an escape room game, but you can set the stage by telling them about an end goal they can reach or an achievement they can earn, such as "train to be a library agent" or "discover the secret of the stacks." Establish a set of tasks for attendees to tackle or determine a list of objects they must find around the library. Or, simply offer them a themed environment to explore and the journey can be the goal. Unlike escape room games, these should be designed to be experienced individually as well as in groups.

SET CHALLENGES

This is your opportunity to provide interaction for your patrons and add a gamification piece to your event. Determine a list of challenges for participants to accomplish at your event. Because you've already established your desired outcomes, you'll know the direction these should go in. If your event is an immersive fan experience such as a Harry Potter Ball or a Star Wars lock-in you can utilize trivia based on the franchise or perhaps a "name that tune" challenge. You could incorporate scavenger hunt and cosplay components, as well as such activities as searching for a hidden lightsaber or having participants create a wand from craft supplies.

If you are hosting a special exhibit, your challenges should be focused on the objects on display. You can quiz participants with riddles based on the knowledge that they've gained by exploring the exhibit. I recently took part in a scavenger hunt that had me explore several local businesses and determine their raison d'etre. Although I realized that this was an obvious way to get me to shop at certain locations, I didn't mind because I was having fun conquering the riddles and challenges in the game. Take advantage of this enjoyable way of learning to get your patrons to discover all that your library has to offer. Instead of giving participants a list of assignments, send them on a quest!

REWARD PARTICIPANTS

What will participants gain by achieving all the tasks or challenges at your event? A sense of fun? The satisfaction of learning something new? How about providing something a little more tangible? Why not present a certificate, a badge, or something else to provide proof that they "won" your scenario, "solved" your crime, or "earned their rank." How about a photo with a prize or integral prop? If you're hosting a scavenger-hunt-style event, what about providing different library stamps that are awarded to participants at different stations around the library? They can earn these from different people whom they locate or for each trivia question they answered correctly. This is your chance to give participants a sense of accomplishment as well as a photo, badge, or other item for bragging rights.

USE TECHNOLOGY

Add some magic to your events by using new technology that will mingle special effects with your library exhibit. You have many choices for this, from creating simple QR codes that can be read with a barcode reader on today's smartphones, to using Bare Conductive's Touch Board for interaction with library displays at your exhibit. See chapter 13 for more on using Arduino boards as well as other cutting-edge technologies for your events.

A popular new technology that museums are using for their exhibits is augmented reality (AR) technology. AR allows you to create images, videos, and text to be superimposed over real-world objects when people wave their phones in front of them. As discussed in chapter 1, I used this at The New York Law Institute to create an augmented reality rare book exhibit. Augmented reality has been brought into the mainstream in recent years with the introduction of games such as Pokemon Go! and others that add a new dimension of interaction with everyday objects. No programming experience is necessary to use this technology.

HP Reveal (www.hpreveal.com), previously known as Aurasma, is a free application that walks you through how to set up augmented reality layers for your desired objects. You create the videos and images that you would like to appear when participants interact with items and then create "auras" or overlays using the application. Once you've uploaded your digital files to the application, HP Reveal will display them in any order you specify. Simply direct your attendees to download the HP Reveal app to their phones and tune into your channel as they enter the event so that they will be able to see all the augmented reality overlays that you have created.

TRY A LARP

LARPs, or live action roleplaying games, are another type of immersive experience that libraries can utilize to engage patrons.

This fantastic walkthrough that details what it takes to host a LARP event in the library was contributed by Tegan Mannino, a technology and technical services librarian at Clapp Memorial Library, Belchertown, Massachusetts.

How to Run a LARP in Your Library

The clock is ticking, you only have thirty minutes to find the disarm code . . .

Pick up your sword and don your armor to face dangers unknown . . .

The dinner party went south when the host showed up dead, now you're trapped in the house and someone (maybe you) is the murderer . . .

Looking in from the outside, the world of immersive play often seems strange, if not confusing and daunting. The most well-known example of immersive play is Live Action Role Play (LARP). The great thing about immersive play is that it does not need to be a huge or unwieldy program but can take place in as little as an hour. You may have already explored this type of play without realizing it.

Immersive play in all its forms asks its participants to interact with setting and narration. They become part of the story, tangibly exploring it. They become invested in the outcome and feel emotions in response to their fictional triumphs and defeats. Libraries, conveniently enough, are full of stories and can create their own places within the stories we tell.

Logistics

Like any program, LARPs take time, space, and support. Figure out what you want to do and what your limitations are. Do you have a budget for the event? What about volunteers who can help? Will this happen during library hours or after, for one hour or the whole day? All the baseline logistics one expects for any event are included in a LARP, with added questions about story and environment. How the pieces come together may vary, with one decision affecting the others.

Will you be the author of the story, or do you want to utilize someone else's work? In addition to asking someone to bring a program to the library, there are a range of commercially available products that may allow you to experiment with forms of immersive play. For murder mysteries, you may have a community member interested in authoring one for an event, or you can investigate the myriad of options online or a "murder mystery in a box" game. For "escape room in a box" options, home games are showing up in major retailer's board game collections, or you can tap into a platform like Breakout EDU, which includes both the hardware and a library of scenarios to run.

What type of event do you want to run? Figure out what story you will tell. This can come from anywhere, maybe a story you've had bouncing around in your head. What is your setting? How does the physical space available affect the program, how can you use it to enhance the story and the mood? You may choose to consider factors such as "out of game" space for your volunteers and staff, where you will store your props and costumes, and where participants can take breaks.

How can you create immersion? When creating the environment look to what you already have on hand before making purchases. You can change the whole look of a room through the use of holiday lights—most people have at least a few sets on hand. Over the past few years a number of incredible free background audio tools for game immersion have emerged, such as Tabletop Audio (https://tabletopaudio.com/), with ambient noise and environmental sound effects that can play on loop in a room. And, if possible, have those helping to put on the event wear costumes. Stepping into a role can be uncomfortable for many people but creating an environment that feels different from everyday allows people to step in to a different role with a lower barrier.

Immersive play runs a gauntlet of options, from short interactions to multi-day events, so you can create an event around what fits within your library and community.

The Story

Start with the story. Everything else flows from it: the characters, the rules, the goals, the entire shape of the event. A LARP is not about "winning," it's about creating a story, asking "yes, and?" Failing a goal should be as much fun for participants as succeeding. Start with a story that appeals to you, be it something you create out of whole cloth, or pull one from a favorite. Another option is to take adventures and campaigns written for established game systems and adapt them to your space and resources.

The beauty of LARP is that the script is thrown out. They say no plan survives contact with the enemy . . . but no carefully constructed plot survives contact with the players!

What you want is a scaffold, an outline for participants to follow. LARP, even when heavily structured, provides sandbox environments for characters to interact with. Build a framework that has the greater shape of the story you wish to tell, decide where you want it to start, and where you would like it to go. Determine actions that will happen regardless of participant action or choice, and what requires specific triggers to occur.

Build out modules (mods), mini-stories, and events that will take place within the greater structure of the event. They can be self-contained or designed to help advance a story. Don't be afraid to create conflicting story lines where one succeeds if another fails. The end should never be completely prewritten. There should be end conditions in place that players are guided towards, but how they discover and interact with the story and its conclusion should be on them.

Time-based triggers are a good way to move things along. Set up elements of the story that occur regardless of action, which allows you to introduce plot elements or create deadlines.

Some starting points for your LARP:

- Escape Rooms

  Escape rooms provide immersion that you can use to build out into a larger story or include as part of your overall event.

- Roleplaying Games

  Roleplaying games (RPGs) may fall on the low end of the immersion scale, but they ask players to engage in creative interaction with a story and shape its direction and outcome. There are extensive libraries of published adventures and campaigns for different settings and rules sets, so you can always borrow and adapt for your LARP.

- Murder Mystery

  Murder mysteries are a sneaky way to introduce LARP; they feel more like a party game but ask players to embrace roles as they explore and interact with the story and each other.

- Live Action Role Play (LARP)

  There are many options, as well as communities that you can tap into or coordinate with. Many existing LARPs can be found across the country. There may be a local LARP ground, such as Ye Olde Commons in Charlton, Massachusetts, where events happen year-round. Organizations such as the Mind's Eye Society have parlor LARP games that take part in an internationally organized story line. Keep an eye out for gaming and fandom conventions, or large production Nordic or Euro-style LARP events in your region.

Characters

Without the characters, the story is just an idea waiting for exploration. Some games invite players to create their own characters, others provide the characters. No matter how characters are handled, make sure to encourage character connections. If players write their own, ask for backstories to be built into connections and goals that prompt interaction with other players and elements of the story.

When writing for Nordic-style LARP, which tends to be much more immersive than other LARP events, I ask players to submit a survey of character traits, preferences, and potential motivations. This is then worked into thumbnail sketches and stories of their characters. The next step from there is to generate connections between different characters, perhaps by setting up a chart and ensuring that everyone has at least one positive connection, one negative connection, and a shared secret, ensuring multiple connections across the board. This encourages character goals and interactions, helping generate a rich story.

Rules of the Game

The focus here is determining how people will interact with the world. Are characters' abilities based on their real-life ability, or do they have special powers and if so, how can they use them?

For example, in combat games, players resolve clashes with physical contact using padded weapons such as "boffers" (https://en.wikipedia.org/wiki/Foam_weapon), or soft projectiles such as nerf darts or "spell packets" (http://larpwiki.labcats.org/index.php?title=Spell_packet). One popular combat rules set used in the northeastern United States is Accelerant, (http://larpwiki.labcats.org/index.php?title=Accelerant) which individual games and campaigns license and modify for their setting. In Nordic or Euro LARP, combat becomes an improv theater exercise, with players relenting to or resisting dramatized attacks. There are countless ways to resolve conflicts and challenges, from those techniques described above to rock/paper/scissors, rolling dice, or other.

The type of story you wish to tell and how you want to tell it will affect the types of challenges the players engage in. Make use of, or create, a rules system that allows you to tell the story.

Doing the Thing

Unusual programs are great ways to draw in new patrons, provided they know about the program. Existing communities that regularly engage in immersive play may already be in your area—the trick will be finding them. Smaller programs like RPGs or escape rooms are often very easy to find players for; because they focus on small groups, and if news gets out into the local community you'll find the sign-up sheets filling up fast. But don't be afraid to advertise in theater groups, gaming or comic book stores, coffee shops, and local schools and colleges.

For larger events like murder mysteries or LARPs, reach out to those same communities for volunteers to help put on the event as well as participants. Volunteers can do more than help set up a space—they can join in the fun by taking on roles and helping build the story and the atmosphere. They also serve as a connection to larger communities from which they can bring in new participants.

Remember to have fun and be open to possibilities. Participants will often find new and inventive ways to explore what you've created, embrace it, and see what comes next.

•••••••

NOTE

1. Ellyssa Kroski, *Cosplay in Libraries: How to Embrace Costume Play in your Library* (Lanham, MD: Rowman and Littlefield, 2015), 41.

9

How to Host a Kid-Friendly Escape Room Event

MANY ESCAPE ROOM GAMES ARE DESIGNED WITH ADULTS AND young adults in mind, but what about children? Kids love to play games and are eager to try their hand at these puzzle-filled, immersive events. What do you need to keep in mind when designing an escape room for children, and what types of learning outcomes can you hope to achieve?

This outstanding project was contributed by East Orange Public Library children's librarians Marissa Lieberman and Lisa O'Shaughnessy.

INTRODUCTION

Your library has decided to host an escape room. Chances are, before you start choosing your story line, making riddles, and creating props, you will first want to decide on your target age group. Although an escape room for children may require more structure than one geared to teens or adults, hosting a library escape room for children can have many benefits. The immersive storytelling experience can promote literacy, problem-solving, and critical thinking in unique and engaging ways. Puzzles can incorporate STEAM, information literacy, or hone fine and gross motor skills. In this chapter, we will provide tips for creating your own kid-friendly escape room, as well as share experiences from our Escape the Fairy Tale event. We encourage you to adapt these tips to meet the needs of your library's space, budget, and patrons.

What's Right for You? Kits versus Building Your Own Story

The decision is made: you're going to create an escape room for children. You've decided on the age group. You may have even picked a date. Great! Now, what's the next step? Where do you begin? Lucky for you, this answer is simple and only involves picking one of two choices. Do you use a premade kit, or will you create your escape room story from scratch?

CHOICE ONE
The Kit

If you have a limited amount of time to plan, not many colleagues who are able to help, or are anxious about how to get started, choosing a kit for a first-time event can be very helpful. The story is already created for you and the puzzles are worked out. Paid-for kits often come with locks, boxes, keys, and props all ready to go. If this sounds right for you, great! The internet is filled with resources waiting to help. There are several companies, such as Breakout EDU, that ship premade kits. Depending on your budget, there are also cheaper downloadable kits. A company called Lock Paper Scissors offers downloadable kits that are ready to play within a very short period of time. Last but not least, there are our DIY friends on the Internet who love to share. If you plug in a search for "DIY escape rooms" you will find a large list of Pinterest, YouTube, and Instructables videos and detailed instructions that will help you get up and running.

CHOICE TWO
Create Your Story from Scratch

Depending on the goals you have for your escape room, creating your own story can have many benefits. Our first goal was to promote literacy. This is why we chose two iconic fairy tales ("Goldilocks and the Three Bears" and "Rumpelstiltskin"). Creating the story, or in our case adapting two well-loved stories, provides flexibility and freedom. You know your audience. You know what will get them excited. Creating the story allows you to immerse them in a narrative experience they will relate to. It also provides the opportunity to introduce new stories they can become excited about. Our second goal was to create an immersive experience by bringing our tales to life. Creating the story allows you the freedom to also create the world it exists in. In *Escape the Fairy Tale,* we had many well-known images to work with, and Goldilocks eating porridge from the Three Bears' bowls to Rumpelstiltskin spinning straw into gold to save the Miller's Daughter. Creating your own props and staging the scenes provides your patrons with a unique experience, unlike in a kit where the props and story are predefined.

Our Story

The fairy narrator explains to the participants in front of the first door: "You are on an adventure through fairyland when you come upon the home of the Three Bears." The doors are flanked by large trees that set the stage of a cottage in the woods. "Goldilocks, however, has already been through the house and messed everything up. She has locked you inside but has left clues for you to find the code to open the lock that will let you escape before the Three Bears return."

As the participants discover the code from the Goldilocks and the Three Bears room, the curtain separating spaces was flung open and the second fairy narrator was revealed. She welcomed her explorers, told them their journey was not complete and guided them into Rumpelstiltskin's world.

> You have entered Rumpelstiltskin's world, where a young woman was forced to spin straw into gold to become queen. As she could not, Rumpelstiltskin appeared to help her and in return for his help she promised him her first-born child. After a year and a day, he returned and told the queen if she could guess his name she could keep her child. The queen could not and Rumpelstiltskin escaped with the child. The knights are out searching for Rumpelstiltskin. Hidden all over are clues to help you escape and help find the child. Start digging.

Riddle Me This

A code is a form of communication, often used to convey a message in a covert way. Letters, numbers, and/or symbols are substituted for one another to disguise a message. Knowing what kind of code is being used, and what the key to decode it is, are necessary for breaking it. You can research different types of codes to use for your escape room or create one yourself. Challenges that require solving a code can be introduced at any time during your program. Codes can allow participants to move from one clue to another or can be used at the end of the room for participants to successfully escape. Codes can be also used in conjunction with other puzzles, word scrambles, hidden text, and locks.

Because our rooms were based on fairy tales, we wanted to use quotes from the text, as well as books from our collection, to help connect the stories to the participants in a way that also made sense for our escape room narrative. In *Escape the Fairy Tale,* we chose to incorporate a combination of codes, riddles, and hidden text. We had two connecting rooms, so we wanted the first room to be a little easier to introduce concepts and strategies participants would later build on in the second room.

In our first room, letters for the alphabet lock code, G-O-L-D, were hidden around parts of the Three Bears' house. Fake clues with pictures of Goldilocks eating porridge, breaking a chair, and sleeping in a bed were also left in these spaces, to throw participants off.

In the Rumpelstiltskin room, each clue was an item or place beginning with one of the letters in the code. In addition, on the wall of names and envelopes, there were several names, objects, and locations that started with one of the letters in the code. Each of these letters was highlighted in a bright color. A riddle was also written on a scroll and placed on the lectern in the throne room: "Instead of my name guess where I may be. These holders of knowledge will give you the key. If you guess correctly you will be set free." The code to escape was B-O-O-K. Rumpelstiltskin was hiding in the library.

Building Your World

Now comes the fun part, bringing your story to life. Whether you've chosen a kit or are building your world from scratch this can be a daunting task. Remember these two simple suggestions and your escape room should be a huge success. First, think about your space critically. What do you have to work with? In our case, we had a large 40' × 30' room with a dividing wall, an immovable stage, recessed lighting, and a projector. Next, after you've thought about your space, walk through it several times to plan out how to stage the scene. Scheduling several planning sessions where we not only talked about what would go in the space, but also walked through the space to map things out, was one of the more productive things we did.

Simple versus Complex

Several things factor into the next portion of your planning process. Planning time, how many staff members are available to help, creative skills, and budget will all dictate whether your world stays simple in its structure or becomes more complex in detail and decoration. For *Escape the Fairy Tale,* we had about a month to plan, two very creative and enthusiastic staff members, and a budget of about $100.00 for two rooms. Although you're creating a world and want that experience to be as immersive as possible, it is important to keep in mind that even the simplest suggestion of your story (e.g., three bowls filled with oats on a table with a tablecloth and vase) will allow your participant's imagination to take over and fill in the gaps.

Setting the Mood: Lighting, Music, Props, and Decoration

Decisions essential for setting the mood or staging your scene include prop placement, what props to make or buy, decorations, mood, lighting, and whether or not to incorporate music. In *Escape the Fairy Tale,* the space used was a 40' × 30' program room. We divided the room into two distinct spaces with the help of a sliding wall. It was important for the participants to feel that the two spaces were completely separate because we were presenting two different but interconnected stories. When they answered the clues from the first story (hidden text, code lock, word scramble) they were transported to a completely different physical space.

In *Goldilocks and the Three Bears,* we incorporated many simple props. To suggest the kitchen, we had a round table with bowls of oats (small, medium, and large), a tablecloth, and vase, along with a kitchen window pasted on the wall. In the living room, we used three chairs from the library (small, medium, and large), a television made of cardboard, toys from storytime, board books from our collection, and family photos of the bears on the wall. In the bedroom, we made three beds (small, medium, and large) out of cardboard, milk crates, and tablecloths. Each area was separate and gave the participants the feeling of traveling through the bears' house.

In *Rumpelstiltskin,* the props were a bit more elaborate, and we employed a change in lighting to further separate the space. When the participants entered the Rumpelstiltskin story, they were in a castle room with dim lighting. In that space was a spinning wheel (made from cheap wood, precut at Home Depot, and a bike wheel borrowed from a friend), two bales of hay, and a chair. Scrolls were also placed on the wall with specific quotes from the story.

After the participants found the clues from the castle room, they entered the throne room by walking through two large Greek columns and down a red carpet. The throne room consisted of a lectern holding the scroll with the most important clue, a throne with two large flag poles, a wall filled with handmade envelopes on decorative paper, and a wall filled with scrolls containing different names. Each prop set the stage in both stories. Whether your props are more elaborate and involve power tools, or less complex and made of cardboard, each can enhance the story in a unique and memorable way.

Collaboration with Your Techie Friends

We all would agree that having friends is a wonderful experience. Your friends expose you to new ideas and ways to see the world and often have skills that complement your own. When building *Escape the Fairy Tale,* we reached out to our tech department to see how they could enhance our fairytale escape room experience. We were able to incorporate sound, and even more exciting, to set up dual webcams to record the experience. So, whether it be your friend Lisa with a power drill, Marissa who has a great narrative mind, or your friend José who can do pretty much anything with a computer, reach out.

Literacy and Empowerment

When planning our first escape room for children, we immediately knew we wanted to bring a story to life by allowing participants to actively engage with literature. We felt fairy tales were the perfect narratives for this goal and included iconic imagery that we could easily replicate in our space. Whether you are bringing a specific tale to life or using another escape scenario, escape rooms expose children to narratives in enjoyable and memorable ways.

Keeping our target audience in mind, we chose to keep our success rate at 100 percent by acting as fairy narrators to guide participants on the right path and ensure everyone escaped. You can change "fairy" to any other character that fits with your scenario, and dressing up as that character adds another fun element to the experience. Creating a safe space for children to solve problems by working together for a common goal builds self-esteem and hones skills needed to succeed in school and life. It is for these reasons that an escape room is a worthwhile program for younger library patrons.

•••••••

10

How to Design a Digital Breakout

A GREAT WAY TO DESIGN ESCAPE GAMES ON THE CHEAP AND increase your ability to accommodate a large crowd is to design a digital breakout. These games are very similar to a physical, live escape room game; however, everything is digital and resides online. These games are incredibly entertaining and an excellent opportunity for learning. Educators and librarians can create them for free using digital tools. The next project will outline what's involved with creating these engaging games.

PLAY A DIGITAL BREAKOUT

If you want to design digital breakouts, start off by playing a few to get an idea of how they are laid out, to see what types of clues are usually used, and to become familiar with the tools involved. I have created a simple digital breakout that you can play at https://sites.google.com/view/draculascurse.

Also, I would recommend going to the Breakout EDU digital sandbox (https://sites.google.com/site/digitalbreakoutjb/sandbox), where you will find over 200 free community-created digital breakouts.

You will notice that the links to the breakouts will lead to either a Google Site or to a website created on Deck Toys (https://deck.toys). These are the two main tools that are currently being used to create these games, with the Google Sites option being the most popular. I will walk you through all you need to know to create your own digital breakout using Google Sites.

MAIN COMPONENTS

There are three main components to designing a digital breakout using Google Sites. They include:

1. **Setting up the lock form.** Just as in a real-life escape room game, you will want to have locks that players must crack in order to advance and win the game.
2. **Developing clues.** You will need to design challenging and appropriate puzzles and clues for players to solve to discover the lock combinations.
3. **Setting up a Google Site.** You will set up a Google Site that is a very basic webpage to display your lock form, information about your breakout game, and links to all your clues.

GETTING STARTED

To begin, think about what you want your learning outcomes to be. Make a bulleted list of these items and they will become your breakout clues and story content. The learning outcomes for my digital breakout based on Bram Stoker's novel *Dracula* included:

- Year published: 1897
- Where Dracula traveled in the novel: London
- Dracula's nemesis: Van Helsing
- Historical figure Dracula is said to have been based on: Vlad the Impaler

Once you have your final results determined, it's easy to start designing your puzzle and the locks.

CREATING YOUR LOCK FORM

Just as in face-to-face escape games, digital breakouts can incorporate several different types of locks. These can be

- Number locks
- Color locks
- Directional locks
- Word locks

After you've decided on your learning outcomes, you can determine what types of locks will best suit your game. From my learning outcomes, I know that I will have the following locks:

- Four-digit number lock (1897)
- Six-digit word lock (London)
- Ten-digit word lock (Van Helsing)
- Seven-digit word lock (Impaler)

To set up a lock form, sign into your Google Drive account. Create a New Folder for your digital breakout. Click into your new folder. Then create a New Form. Name the form "[Your Breakout Title] Lock Form."

For each of the questions on your form, define the type of lock. For example, my first question on my form is "Four-Digit Number Lock" (see figure 10.1). Keep the question type the default Short Answer. Choose the answer parameters to be Text;Contains "[Type the correct answer]." Then add an error message for players who enter the wrong combination. I chose to use "Try Again!" Be sure to make the question Required. Click on the three dots at the bottom of the question to select more options. Be sure to check Response Validation so that the form will not let the player proceed with an incorrect answer, and also "Description" if you are including a description.

Include descriptive instructions with complex locks such as a Five-Digit Directional Lock question. This could include instructions such as U up, D Down, L Left, R Right (ALL Caps, No Spaces). If you'd like to preview your Lock form at any time, click the icon of the eye on the top of the website.

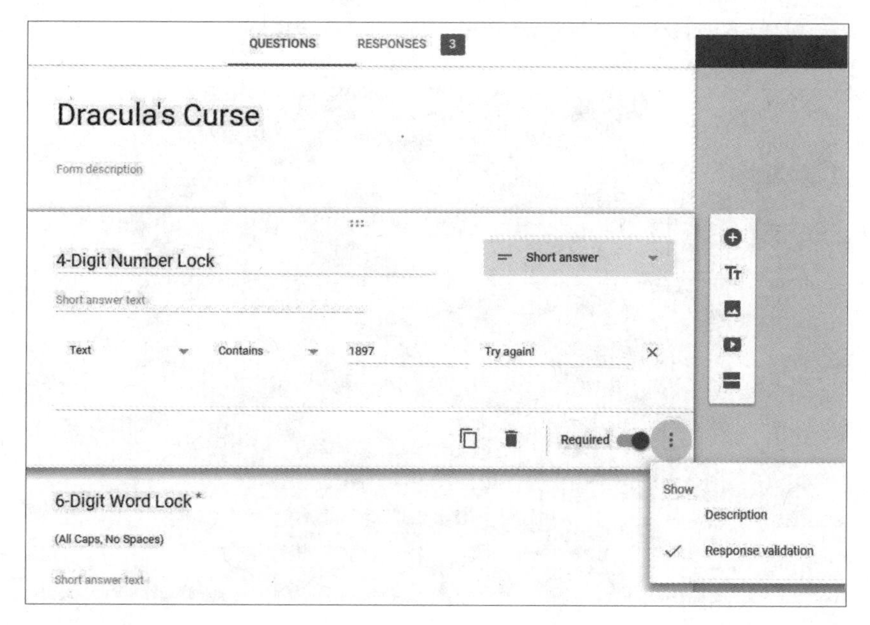

FIGURE 10.1

Google Form lock form for a digital escape game

Once you're done with your first question, use the Duplicate option at the bottom to create your next lock with all the settings already applied. Before you finish, click the Settings icon of the gear at the top of the page and select Presentation. Change the Confirmation Message from the default "Your response has been recorded" to something like "CONGRATULATIONS, you solved the Breakout!"

Google Drive automatically saves your form as you create it, so once you're done with your form, you will find it in your digital breakout folder.

CREATING YOUR CLUES

There are many different ways that you can provide clues and pathways for your breakout players. Many of those discussed in earlier chapters can be used and linked within these digital versions of escape games. Here are a few more ideas.

Create a Custom Google Drawing for a Jigsaw Puzzle

One puzzle type that is frequently used in digital breakouts is the jigsaw puzzle clue. It is quite simple to create your own graphic using a Google Drawing to create the basis for your jigsaw puzzle. Select New→Google Drawing. Find an

FIGURE 10.2
Dracula jigsaw puzzle created at Jigsaw Planet

image or combine several images you'd like to use and add them to the drawing. Use the handles on the images to resize them. Add a background color by right-clicking on the drawing. And add any text you'd like to add to your clue. For my puzzle I found a Wikipedia image of Vlad, inserted the image, added a black background color, and added the text underneath "Vlad the ________" in order to lead players to the seven-digit word lock answer.

Once you've created your Google Drawing, select File→ Download As→ jpg. Next go to Jigsaw Planet at https://www.jigsawplanet.com and click Create at the top of the site. Upload your file. I chose to keep mine on the default Easy setting of thirty-five pieces, but you can adjust this as you like. I also chose to stay with the classic, default jigsaw puzzle shape, shown in figure 10.2. Click Create.

To be able to share your puzzle in your breakout, be sure to copy the link to your puzzle.

Create a Google Form to Quiz Players

You can create Google Forms in order to quiz your players on a specific topic area or subject. Simply follow the same instructions as you did when you created your lock form. Because you'll be making all your questions Required and selecting Response Validation, the only way for players to Submit the form is to have all the correct responses filled in. Therefore, you can end the quiz with a Confirmation Message to provide players with a lock combination or further clues. For example, you can create a quiz of four or five questions based on your topic area that players need to answer correctly to get the confirmation message "RBYGY," which could unlock a five-digit color lock if you choose to include one.

OTHER PUZZLES

In addition to these puzzle suggestions, you have many options for building your own puzzles. Many puzzle and clue creation sites have been collected into a community-sourced document available at https://sites.google.com/site/digitalbreakoutjb/how-to. This massive list contains tools for creating your own challenges and clues, including

- An airline ticket generator
- A newspaper clipping generator
- A fake phone text generator
- A jigsaw puzzle creator
- A fake receipt creator
- A fake concert ticket generator

Other ideas for puzzles might be[1]

- Linking to articles or videos online that might reveal something about your breakout.
- Designing a custom Google Map to give directional clues.
- Creating additional Google Sites subpages with riddles and puzzles that are linked from your main Google Site.

For my digital breakout, I chose to create one puzzle within a newspaper clipping using the newspaper generator with the words "(Year)" and "(Published)" hidden within the text. I also set the date of the newspaper the same as the novel publication year. Many of these games will hide a shortened URL such as a bit.ly URL address within blocks of text by bolding letters that players need to put together to form the complete URL string. I took the image of my newspaper clipping, placed it within a Google Drawing, made the sharing options on the Drawing viewable by everyone on the Web, and added it to my Hotspot Drawing (see instructions below). This provides the answer to my four-digit number lock.

I also created a word puzzle similar to an anagram on the Discovery Education website located here: www.discoveryeducation.com/free-puzzlemaker. As with the previous clue, I inserted the image of the word puzzle into a Google Drawing, made it shareable, and linked to it on my Google Site within my Hotspot Drawing. Solving this double word puzzle provides players with the ten-digit word lock answer: "Van Helsing."

For my final puzzle I created a Match the Memory game in which players are challenged to match cards with images of the actors who have portrayed Dracula over the years in a memory-style game available here: https://matchthememory.com/Dracula. Winners receive a message with the clue: "City Dracula traveled to in the novel," which reveals the six-digit word lock answer "London."

SETTING UP YOUR GOOGLE SITE

To bring all of this together you will want to create a Google Site page to present all of these puzzles to your players. From Google Drive select New→ Google Site. Start by adding your breakout title and change the header image to one that fits your motif. Choose Insert on the right and add a Text Box right underneath the header image. Here's where you can add a description of your game, what it's about, what the players need to do, and so on. If you'd like to preview your site at any time, click the icon of the eye on the top of the website.

On the right, select Themes and choose from many different themes to suit your taste. Next, choose Insert and select From Google Drive. Open your breakout folder that you set up for this digital game, select your lock form, and click on Insert at the bottom. Drag it to the left side of your page, underneath the header image.

Next, you will choose how you will present your clues and puzzles to your players. You can create a text box with a list of links to all the puzzles that you've created to the right side of your lock form as one option. Another option might be to create additional pages on your Google Site by clicking on the right on the Pages tab and selecting +Add Page at the bottom. One frequently used method for these digital breakouts is to create an image using a Google Drawing with embedded links (called hotspots) that lead players to the puzzles and clues.

CREATE A GOOGLE DRAWING WITH HOTSPOTS

In Google Drive, select New→Google Drawing. Choose an image to feature as a main part of your breakout, then upload it and insert it into your Google Drawing. Next you can add links within your image so that when players click on certain areas of the image, they will be brought to your puzzles. To do that, you will add shapes to your image. Select the Shapes tool on the toolbar and add whatever shape you would like to your image and resize and position it. Next, with the shape still selected, set the Fill Color and the Border Color to Transparent using the options on the toolbar at the top of the Google Drawing. You will also select the Link icon and insert a link to one of your puzzles. You can continue to do this using the Shapes tool to draw various shapes throughout your drawing until all your puzzles are linked. You may also choose to insert other images on top of your main image in order to hyperlink them.

When you set up this Google Drawing, it is very important that you make it viewable by everyone on the web so that your players will have access to it. The default privacy setting for Google Drawings is that they are viewable only by the creator. On the top right of your Google Drawing, click on the Share button with the padlock. Select Advanced on the bottom right. Look for the section that says, "Who Has Access." Click on Change next to Private—Only You Can Access. Here you can turn on link sharing by choosing "On—Public on the Web," this will let anyone on the internet view your drawing without signing into Google. You will need to duplicate this procedure for any puzzles you created using Google Drawings to which you plan to link directly within your game.

After you have completed your Hotspot Drawing, go back to your Google Site and select Insert→ From Google Drive and find it within your folder. Drag your hyperlinked Drawing to the right of your Lock form on your page. Now your breakout players should have all that they need to crack the game. Next, publish your Google Site so that it's viewable by the public. This option is on the top right of your site. Click on Publish and choose a name for your breakout URL.

TEST YOUR GAME

Before giving out the URL for your digital breakout game, be sure to test out all the components you created to make sure that everything is working properly. The first step for this procedure is to sign yourself out of Google. None of your players will be signed into your account so you want to be sure to see what they'll see while you're testing. The point of testing is to make sure that everyone has access to all the forms and documents you created as well as to test out all the hyperlinks you created.

MORE RESOURCES

There are many video tutorials for how to set up digital breakouts on the Breakout EDU website at https://sites.google.com/site/digitalbreakoutjb/how-to. Educator Meagan Kelly has put together an excellent video tutorial on how to set up a digital breakout (https://www.youtube.com/watch?v=hZu4BTUAGW8) and teacher April Whitehead has created a very clear video walk-through of how to set up digital locks using Google Forms (https://youtu.be/Fd0CZaSWPjA).

You may also choose to use a different technology to create your digital breakout such as Deck Toys (https://deck.toys) or the Room Escape Maker (http://doctorfou.com/room-escape-maker).

NOTE

1. Brynn Allison, "Resources for Creating Digital Breakouts: Ideas for Making Your Own Activities," *The Literary Maven,* April 29, 2017, https://www.theliterarymaven.com/2017/04/breakout-digital-escape-room-ideas.html.

11

All About Escape Room Board Games

BOARD GAMES ARE BIG IN LIBRARIES AND PATRONS LOVE THEM. They are a vehicle to foster social interaction and a sense of community as well as to encourage strategic and critical-thinking skills. And they are a hit with people of all ages. They can be used to engage library patrons at a variety of different library events including board game nights, summer reading events, and gaming days; as a part of library lock-in events; or as an alternative activity within larger events such as comic cons or anime events.[1]

Escape room board games bridge the gap between hosting a full escape room event and presenting a board game night. They provide the same sorts of puzzles and challenges that can be found in escape rooms and can accommodate a similarly sized group of participants. Games can be purchased from online retailers such as Amazon.com for prices ranging from $15 to $40.

The same types of considerations should be taken into account when selecting escape room board games for the library's collection as would be considered for other materials. A budget should be set, and an acquisitions policy should be developed that includes criteria such as target audience, price range, number of players, and noise levels. Carli Spina offers some great tips in "Bring Board Games to Your Library: Collection Development Tips and Best Practices." You may also want to have a look at the acquisitions criteria for the circulating board games collection for the Bucks County (Pennsylvania) Library System (http://bit.ly/2FBKZlF).[2]

An excellent resource for selecting board games is the website BoardGame Geek (https://boardgamegeek.com). This essential resource provides information and reviews about almost every board game in existence as well as user ratings and forums with helpful community-provided information.

ESCAPE ROOM BOARD GAME RECOMMENDATIONS

There are many escape room-style board games available on websites such as Amazon and in stores such as Books-A-Million, Walmart, and Barnes and Noble. Here are a few recommendations to get you started.

ESCAPE THE ROOM

Secret of Dr. Gravely's Retreat

Age:	13+
Number of Players:	Three to eight
Playing Time:	90 minutes
Price:	$21.99
Where to Purchase:	Amazon.com
Difficulty:	Beginner/Intermediate
Replay Value for Libraries:	Excellent

Thinkfun, an educational board game company, currently offers two excellent escape room board games, the more challenging of which is *The Secret of Dr. Gravely's Retreat*.

The game transports players to the year 1913, when they have won a free stay at the Foxcrest Retreat run by the famous Dr. Gravely. But this spa retreat is not what it seems—and may not turn out to be all that healthy. Players must discover the dark secret of Dr. Gravely's retreat so that they can escape before time runs out.

The game comes fully assembled with an instruction booklet, four envelopes that contain the main puzzles of the game and story cards, and a solution wheel that tells players if they have solved a challenge. Players work together, and as each puzzle is successfully solved they are given access to more envelopes and further challenges. Puzzles come in a variety of types and materials are made of high-quality materials.

Although this game can be played by as many as eight players, it is recommended for fewer players or for teams of players because several parts of the game can only be played by one person at a time. This is an excellent choice for libraries that appeals to a wide range of players and age levels. It also has excellent replay value, although the same group of players will not want to replay the game once they have solved the puzzles within; none of the pieces of the game will be damaged or written on during gameplay so the library can reuse the game many times. Thinkfun also provides outstanding reassembly instructions on its website.[3]

ESCAPE THE ROOM
Mystery at the Stargazer's Manor

Age:	10+
Number of Players:	Three to eight
Playing Time:	90 minutes
Price:	$21.99
Where to Purchase:	Amazon.com
Difficulty:	Beginner
Replay Value for Libraries:	Excellent

Also from Thinkfun Games, this beginner escape game is sure to please first-time players and escape room novices.

It's the year 1869 and the town astronomer has gone missing since the death of his wife. Yet his manor house has been anything but quiet. Villagers have heard loud noises coming from the estate and have noticed smoke billowing from the observatory. Players must work together to solve the *Mystery at the Stargazer's Manor* and save the astronomer.

This game is set up in much the same way as *Dr. Gravely's Retreat*, with five sealed envelopes containing puzzles and secret items, an instruction booklet, and a solution wheel. This is also a cooperative play game in which all players team up to solve the mystery. The challenges posed come in a variety of types and materials are high-quality.

This game is also recommended for play with fewer than the maximum eight players and would likely be best with a maximum of four due to the ease of the puzzles. This is another great choice for libraries because of its wide appeal and replay value. And just as with *Dr. Gravely's Retreat*, the Thinkfun website provides excellent reassembly instructions for repackaging the game.[4]

ESCAPE ROOM IN A BOX

The Werewolf Experiment Game

Age:	13+
Number of Players:	Two to eight
Playing Time:	30–90 minutes
Price:	$29.99
Where to Purchase:	Amazon.com
Difficulty:	Intermediate
Replay Value for Libraries:	Excellent

Upon opening the box, players are exposed to a werewolf toxin released by a mad scientist. Players must work cooperatively to solve all the puzzles and unlock the antidote hidden within the crazed doctor's laboratory or be forever transformed into werewolves.

Originally started via a Kickstarter campaign, this Mattel game comes fully assembled with an instruction guide. It is unique for a number of reasons. It comes with nineteen engaging puzzles of a variety of types including codes to decipher, clues to find, and physical puzzles. Also included are three locked items secured by actual locks for players to open. In addition to the use of real locks and complex puzzles, this game sets itself apart by integrating the use of Amazon's Alexa device. Although not required to play the game, hosts may choose to have Alexa keep time, provide hints, and play a suspenseful soundtrack during the game.

The game can be played with two to eight players who can take on puzzles individually and then rejoin the cooperative play. This is an excellent choice for libraries as all the members of a large group can play at the same time, and because its puzzles are of varying degrees of difficulty and provide something for everyone. It also has excellent replay value. The game's website provides detailed repacking instructions and downloadable files to print items consumed in the game.

ESCAPE ROOM

The Game

Age:	16+
Number of Players:	Three to five
Playing Time:	60 minutes
Price:	$39.99
Where to Purchase:	Amazon.com
Difficulty:	Beginner/Intermediate
Replay Value for Libraries:	Excellent

Escape Room The Game from Spin Master Games is a set of four 60-minute escape rooms based on different scenarios. Included in the box are all the puzzles, clues, cards, and instructions to play *Prison Break, Virus, Nuclear Countdown,* and *Temple of the Aztec* escape games.

The game comes fully assembled with four envelopes containing all the components for the individual escape games. The box also comes with a large timer on the Chrono Decoder device that counts down from 60 minutes, which makes the experience seem more like an actual escape room. Players must work together to solve all the puzzles within the three stages of each scenario and can use the hint decoder to get help when needed.

This is a great choice for libraries because it has multiple games in one box. It also has excellent replay value for future groups wishing to play. The website provides downloadable and printable puzzle components for each scenario. This game also has several expansion packs available to supplement the core game with the Chrono Decoder. Additional expansion packs include:

- *Funland*
- *Murder Mystery*
- *Virtual Reality* (which comes with VR glasses)

EXIT THE GAME
The Abandoned Cabin

Age:	12+
Number of Players:	One to four
Playing Time:	1–2 hours
Price:	$14.95
Where to Purchase:	Amazon.com
Difficulty:	Intermediate
Replay Value for Libraries:	Not good

This series of games by Thames and Kosmos consists of ten escape board games from Germany, many of which are award-winning, and all of which are available in English. They each involve placing the player in a menacing escape scenario such as this first in the series, *The Abandoned Cabin*. Players find themselves taking shelter for the night in an abandoned cabin in the woods after their car breaks down. But upon waking up in the morning they discover that the door has been locked and there are bars on the windows. Can players work together to solve the riddles left for them by their captor in order to escape the cabin?

Each game comes fully assembled with a decoder disk, three decks of cards including Riddle, Help, and Answer decks; various strange items; and an instruction booklet. All materials in these games are of high quality; however, a drawback of these games is that they require players to fold, write on, and sometimes tear the puzzle pieces to solve the game. The back of the game boxes does warn purchasers that games can be played only once due to this design choice. However, users have found that it is possible to reassemble and repackage these games for replay by doing a little bit of preparation. Tips and guides for making most of these games replayable can be found on the BoardGameGeek website within the forums for most of the individual games. Librarians will want to check out these pages beforehand and plan on doing some preparation such as making photocopies of puzzle elements before releasing these games to patrons. Other games in this series include:

- *Exit: The Polar Station*
- *Exit: The Secret Lab*
- *Exit: The Sinister Mansion*
- *Exit: The Sunken Treasure*
- *Exit: Dead Man on the Orient Express*
- *Exit: The Forbidden Castle*
- *Exit: The Mysterious Museum*
- *Exit: The Pharaoh's Tomb*
- *Exit: The Forgotten Island*

NOTES

1. John Pappas, "Board in the Library, Part One: An Introduction to Designer Board Games," *WebJunction,* December 30, 2013, https://www.webjunction.org/news/webjunction/board-in-the-library-part-one.html.
2. Carli Spina, "Bring Board Games to Your Library: Collection Development Tips and Best Practices," *CCGC in Libraries,* April 13, 2015, http://ccgclibraries.com/bring-board-games-to-your-library-collection-development-tips-and-best-practices/; John Pappas, "Program Model: Circulating Board Game Collection," *Programming Librarian,* February 2, 2017, www.programminglibrarian.org/programs/circulating-board-game-collection.
3. William Chen and Yuan Jiang, Review of "*The Secret of Dr. Gravely's Retreat*—Thinkfun," *Escape Room Tips,* October 4, 2016, https://escaperoomtips.com/product/secret-dr-gravelys-retreat-Thinkfun-review.
4. William Chen and Yuan Jiang, Review of "*The Mystery at the Stargazer's Manor*—Thinkfun," *Escape Room Tips,* October 4, 2016, https://escaperoomtips.com/product/mystery-stargazers-manor-Thinkfun.

12

How to Host an Escape Room Event for Team-Building and Staff Training

AS DISCUSSED IN EARLIER CHAPTERS, ESCAPE ROOM GAMES are an outstanding medium for facilitating team bonding, cooperation, and learning. They are consistently used by major corporations for staff team-building events and by educators who wish to impart lessons to students in a gamified manner. They are excellent vehicles for library staff training and team-building, and they are eagerly anticipated experiences rather than avoided or suffered through as are many workshops.

• •

Susan Mythen, a librarian at Florida State College at Jacksonville, has contributed this excellent project detailing how to utilize escape room games as tools for staff team-building.

Designing Staff Team-Building Escape Rooms

Escape rooms can be an excellent team-building experience. An escape room that is designed to appeal to multiple competencies and that plays to the strengths of its diverse team members can break down barriers and bring individuals together in pursuit of a common goal. Escape room activities do not need to be hugely thematic, and do not require the type of Hollywood set-decoration skills we sometimes see in commercial escape rooms. Instead, libraries that want to build cohesive teams can use simple escape games that require participants to work together to solve problems, relying on each other's strengths to break out together.

Our college recently held its first Library and Learning Commons Staff Development Day. Our institution has seven locations: four main campuses and three centers. Many of our staff members from one location had never met a single employee from another campus. We utilized an escape room as a team-building exercise as a vehicle for all the library and learning commons employees to get together and get to know their counterparts that worked at other campus locations.

This type of event easily translates to other types of libraries as well. Public libraries have multiple branches within a city or county, and include varied departments such as youth services, reference, and technical services. School libraries are spread out within a school district, but they share common goals and services. Library employees are often put into arbitrary groups based on job title or job classification: librarians, paraprofessionals, faculty, staff, administrators, and so on. An escape room activity can offer the chance for all these groups to work together.

Organizing the Event

Our event included about seventy participants who were broken into two competing teams. But no matter how many participants you have, you can divide them into teams that will take on the escape room challenge together. Each team should work in a separate room with its own facilitator to monitor the activities and provide hints as needed. You can use classrooms, meeting rooms, conference rooms, or any type of space that is available in your event location. The only room requirement is a few tables on which to place the printed materials and the props for the game. The actual doors to the meeting rooms do not need to be locked. You'll just need to organize your event so that the teams simply need to unlock the final box to gain the message that is locked inside, rather than break out of a room.

You can purchase an escape room lock kit from Breakout EDU that will include all the materials needed for your activity, but locks and other items can easily be purchased locally or ordered online. Our game used the following items:

- small box with hasp
- large box with hasp
- three-digit lock
- four-digit lock
- directional lock
- key lock
- color-coded lock

It is important to note the usefulness of having a small locking box as well as a large one. The game should be constructed so that the first and easiest code to break is the three-digit lock on the small box. This gives the players a few small victories: knowing where to start, unlocking something for a sense of accomplishment, and getting more tools and clues from inside the small box. In our game, there was a QR code taped to the outside of the small locked box. Someone on the team just needed to figure out that they should scan the QR code with a participant's phone to get a message, which led to a clue that revealed a three-digit number. The three-digit number then opened that smaller box, which held a black-light flashlight and a chart used for another code. This is a system that we have been able to use over and over again as we create new games for student groups and classes. Although we don't always start the game with a QR code, we know that we need to design the activity so that the first item that players crack is the small box.

Choosing the Game

Keep in mind that members of your teams may be diverse, ranging from math tutors and managers to library assistants and deans. When deciding on the theme for this activity, you want to be careful not to alienate any one group by having its title mention "library," "math," or anything else too specific. You may prefer to choose a game with a more subject-neutral theme such as "the faculty meeting" that will be broad enough to appeal to all participants. There are hundreds of free escape room games available online; this one can be downloaded with all instructions included from the Breakout EDU website (https://platform.BreakoutEDU.com/game/the-faculty-meeting).[1]

Within *The Faculty Meeting* game itself are activities that require using such reference materials as a dictionary, science texts, and a book of quotations; math skills such as *x* and *y* coordinates; chemical element information such as a periodic table that will be available in the room; and other simple academic tasks. This is a perfect way to bring diverse professionals together and keep all on equal footing. And this is something that is easily tailored to the strengths and backgrounds of your own group.

Adding a Twist

A twist to consider adding to your team-building escape game is requiring competing teams to share some piece of information with each other in order to complete their task. Perhaps one group's key fits the lock in the other room, and vice versa. Perhaps there is a four-digit code, but the group only has three of the digits. This is a good twist to add if you have experienced team members who have done escape rooms before (they won't be expecting this!) or if you have a very competitive group that needs to emphasize teamwork and cooperation. Remember that the facilitators will always know how to steer the group toward completion, so there shouldn't be any worries that participants will get to the point of frustration. Instead, this is an excellent live-action illustration of the importance of communication and cooperation between locations, departments, and teams.

The Debrief

Packaged escape room games typically come with reflection activities or discussion questions that can be explored at the end of the event. This "debriefing" can be one of the most important learning activities, so don't skip it. Here are a few questions to consider asking your participants:

How did you feel during this activity?
Did you feel valued and included?
What was the most stressful part?
What was the most satisfying part?
How did you contribute to the team?
How was your team's communication?
What was the most effective strategy your team used?
What would you do differently next time?
What did you learn from this exercise?

Escape room activities are an entertaining and effective way to break the ice, build community, and bridge divides. Players are required to communicate with each other and work toward a common goal, which requires all members to listen, speak up, and actively participate. The end-of-game reflection gives players the chance to evaluate their own participation and see how they contributed to the group. Facilitators have the chance to steer the reflective conversation toward the goals of the organization and emphasize how each player is a valued member of the library team.

•••••••

Mackenzie Morning, access services manager at Winona State University's Darrell W. Krueger Library, offers these three helpful tips for organizing staff-training escape games.

ADVICE FOR CREATING AND USING BREAKOUTS FOR TRAINING PURPOSES

1. **Take stock.** Make sure you know what you want or need your training to cover and then decide if those tasks or policies would be appropriate for an escape room. It is also important to take stock in order to know what you are working with as far as supplies go. Whether you have a Breakout EDU kit, your own homemade version, or even just office supplies, all of these will work to create an escape room. Do you have a budget to purchase materials? Along with this, be aware of how much time you will still have to create the escape room. Finally, know what you bring to the table and work from your strengths, whether they are your crafting or technological skills.
2. **Be creative.** You need to create a story line, clues, and answers that fit both your story and your training subject along with at least a few false positives to make it more challenging. You will also need to gather and assemble any props. This is where you will spend the majority of your time. It is easy run out of time in this stage and be tempted to skip the trial run. Do not do that.
3. **Do a trial run.** First walk yourself through it, but then have a group test your escape room scenario. Things that make sense to you will not necessarily be clear to the test group. After watching the test group, ask them questions about their experience. Take this feedback and adjust if necessary.

Overall, making sure that the material fits an escape room and performing trial runs are the two best and most important pieces of advice I can give. If the material does not fit an escape room setting or a clue does not work because you skipped a trial run, then it is a wasted opportunity and ineffective for training.

NOTE

1. You must create a free account to access this and other free games on Breakout EDU.

13

How to Add a High-Tech Twist to Your Escape Room

THERE ARE MANY DIFFERENT TYPES OF TECHNOLOGY, FROM Arduino boards that provide audio special effects to robots that will walk a maze to reveal a lock combination, which you can add to your escape room to ensure an "ahh!" response from players. These types of surprises will add mystery and magic to your room and make the experience exceptionally memorable for your players.

> It's that magic factor. As mainstream as it's become—everybody's got a smartphone these days, everybody's got a good computer and a good internet connection—there is still that magical nature to some tech, especially when you use it in unexpected ways.[1]

Juan Denzer, discovery services librarian at the SUNY Oswego Penfield Library, offers this outstanding collection of nine high-tech projects (seven plus two bonus projects) detailing the many ways to utilize cutting-edge technology in your escape games.

Technology and Escape Games

Escape rooms are a great place for puzzle-solving using makerspace technology. Circuit boards, LEDs, LCDs, servos, and so on, are all part a DIY hacker's toolbox. These tools can be easily used to develop fun and exciting puzzles for an escape room. Technology allows you to go beyond the traditional lock-and-key or combination to open a puzzle. The following do-it-yourself projects are designed to be simple enough for any library to implement. The projects range from beginner to intermediate. They use a combination of high-tech to low-tech materials. Many of the projects can be created with makerspace materials you may already have in your library. The first five projects cost between $50 to $100, while the last few range between $100 to $200. Each project is designed to be customized. This allows libraries to recycle the project just by changing the content.

Once the technology of the project is completed, the content can be changed with little to no reconfiguration of the hardware. The projects can be tools for the librarian's DIY toolbox that will allow librarians to change puzzles and make their escape rooms fresh. The projects are also low maintenance, which is important when creating and maintaining escape rooms.

The projects are listed from beginner to intermediate:

- Project 1: Circuit-building puzzle
- Project 2: "Where's Waldo" puzzle
- Project 3: Follow the maze
- Project 4: Play "Twinkle, Twinkle, Little Star" puzzle
- Project 5: Crack a Morse code puzzle
- Project 6: "Look mom, no hands!" game
- Project 7: Use "The Force" maze

Special Components: Projects 2 to 5 use a specific Arduino-based board called a Bare Conductive Touch Board. Even though the projects call for this board, they can also use any Arduino board. The Bare Conductive Touch Board retails for $69.99. The board is a Leonardo-based Arduino. It was chosen for these projects for its compact form and ease of use. The board can function just like other Arduinos. It incorporates touch and mp3 playback technology into the board. This allows anyone to use it right out of the box without any need to program it. Other advanced functions will require some programming knowledge. (Details are available at www.bareconductive.com/shop/touch-board).

Projects 6 and 7 will require a device called Leap Motion, which retails for $79.99. The Leap Motion is a USB controller that connects to any computer. It is a gesture-recognition device that can be programmed to manipulate programs with hand and other fine gestures. (Details are available at www.leapmotion.com).

Project 7 uses a robotic ball called Sphero. This ball can be controlled using Bluetooth enabled devices, such as a smartphone. The Sphero Education and Sphero Mini retails for $129.99 and $49.99, respectively. (Details are available at www.sphero.com).

PROJECT 1
Circuit-Building Puzzle

This project is the easiest one to implement. Even though the project is simple, it does not mean it is not an effective and challenging puzzle. Materials required can be as minimal as an Arduino, LED, diode, and wires.

Begin by choosing a circuit that is easy to wire on a breadboard. The official Arduino site (www. Arduino.cc) is a great place to find simple tutorials. The tutorials give detailed instructions, code, and diagrams. The wiring diagrams are what make the projects visually appealing and effective.

Once you have decided on a circuit, implementation is simple. Download and print the wire diagram in color. Create step-by-step instructions on how to wire the circuit. Mount the Arduino and breadboard holder (e.g., this one https://www.sparkfun.com/products/11235). Display the diagram and instructions next to the Arduino and components. Some examples of what occurs when circuits are completed include:

- A circuit that lights an LED. This LED is used to illuminate a hidden code.
- A circuit that plays a sound. The sound could be a combination that unlocks a box.
- A circuit that triggers a switch. The switch can be used to unlock a door or box. The switch can be used to turn on a light or play a device.
- A circuit that triggers a servo. The servo can be connected to a flag that pops up with a code or message.

The circuit-building puzzles use inexpensive Arduino boards that and many library makerspaces already own. In recent years two products designed to teach STEM have become popular: littleBits (littlebits.cc) and Snap Circuits (elenco.com). What makes them a great alternative to Arduinos and breadboards is their simplicity to connect circuits.

LittleBits use a color-coded system to identify components. Instead of using breadboards and wires, littleBits uses magnets to connect each component. The polarity of each magnet is placed in such a way that circuits cannot be wired incorrectly. This makes it easier to connect circuits. This system is great for accessibility in escape rooms, especially when the rooms are designed for smaller children. The color-coded magnetic system is less intimidating than traditional boards and breadboards.

A group of students from Reading College in the United Kingdom created larger littleBits using 3-D printers (extrasensoryobjects.wordpress.com/2013/12/06/littlebits-go-large). They wanted to make them easier to handle. The littleBits components are mounted on 3-D printed bases. The system follows the same design as the original. This upgrade would be perfect for this project. It makes the components more assessable for all ages.

Snap Circuits is another STEM teaching system. Unlike littleBits, this system uses a grid similar to a breadboard. The circuits "snap" into place using snap-type fasteners, which makes it is easy to connect circuits. It has a slight level of complexity as circuits must be snapped correctly. The system does not use magnets to ensure proper connection.

PROJECT 2
"Where's Waldo" Puzzle

This project uses capacitive touch technology, the same technology used in smartphones. Capacitive touch uses the body's electricity to register an event. (This is not to be confused with resistive touch, which uses mechanical components to trigger an event.) Capacitive touch is preferred because it does not require any special film or components. Almost any material can be used including wood, plastic, paper, metal, or fabric. This project requires a Bare Conductive Touch Board, painting or printed image, picture frame, conductive paint or shielded wire, and a power source.

Start by selecting a painting or a printed image. Choose an image that has lots of objects and color. A good example would be a painting of a baseball game. The goal is to choose a specific object or area in the image. Then clues will be given to find the object. Just as in project 1, the trigger will activate an event, which could be a code combination or opening a lock.

After the image is selected, mount it to a cardboard back. On the back of the cardboard mark the location of the object by drawing a circle around it. Make sure the area selected measures about three fingers in diameter. Anything smaller might be too difficult to find in a large print. Once done, add a frame to your print.

After the print is framed, it is time to wire the circuit. Using conductive paint, paint in the circle on the back of the cardboard. Draw a circuit line to one end of the frame. Wire can be used as substitution. Place a piece of wire at the ending point of the image and connect it to the touch board. Make sure to add a trigger event such as in project 1. Finally, add a power source and the project is ready to be displayed. An in-depth tutorial on how to wire graphics with the touch board is available at www.bareconductive.com/make/starter-project-1-graphic-sensors.

PROJECT 3
Follow the Maze Puzzle

This project is a variation of project 2. The set-up is almost identical but adds a twist that can be accomplished with some extra coding of the touch board. The layout uses a maze. There are several online sites such as www.mazegenerator.net that will generate a maze and solution. Choose one that is an intermediate level.

Follow the steps from project 2 to create the puzzle. The trick to making this work involves using several points rather than a single point. Using only one point, the end, would be pointless because a user could just touch that point. To ensure the user is actually trying to solve the maze, include a few key points that the user must touch (e.g., an important turn in the maze).

Once the points are selected, painted, and wired to the touch board, you will need to write code that follows the sequence of touches. The first point should be set as the reset trigger and the last point as the finishing trigger. Any points that are touched out of sequence will register as failures and reset the maze. You can add color LEDs or a buzzer to indicate if the progress is a correct or a failed attempt. If you want to make the maze even more challenging, you can add fault triggers to dead ends. Many mazes will lead to a dead end as part of the challenge. The puzzle can be coded so that a dead-end touch triggers an immediate reset.

PROJECT 4
Play "Twinkle, Twinkle, Little Star" Puzzle

This project can easily be constructed by following the video tutorial at https://www.youtube.com/watch?v=qtDZ3fYyUNO. How could you use it in an escape room project? Use it to play a few bars of music. This is a great way to introduce users to reading music. You don't have to make them play a concerto, but it is fun to give them a taste of playing a musical instrument. The end trigger can be just like those in the other projects listed above. For an added twist, try adding a dramatic "dun dun dun" sound. This can add an amusing effect when a user fails.

PROJECT 5
Crack a Morse Code Puzzle

Following project 5, the Morse code puzzle is a great way to teach someone a little Morse code. An Arduino is a great board to make a Morse code transmitter. It can transmit a flashing LED or sound. Here is the code for the classic "Hello World." It uses an LED connected to the proper pin to transmit. This code can easily be modified to transmit a sound instead. To make it simpler to read, you can add different color lights to signal the end of a word or a specific sound.

For an added twist, you can design the transmitter to use an LED. Have the user access a decoder app that will decipher Morse code. You can also turn the concept around and have the user send a coded message via smartphone and have an Arduino read it. User Hackertje at instructables.com has created a project that uses an Arduino to read a Morse code input and display it on an LCD (www.instructables.com/id/Arduino-Morse-Decoder/). This variation can add a trigger to an event. If the user sends the correct code, the trigger fires. If the code is wrong, the trigger sends a "failed "message.

PROJECT 6
"Look Mom, No Hands!" Game

This project breaks away from the use of Arduino boards. Instead it uses a traditional laptop or computer. The key piece of hardware is a Leap Motion controller (www.leapmotion.com), which allows a user to manipulate a program with hand gestures. The Leap Motion is capable of registering gestures down to the fingers. This project uses the controller to navigate a video game.

Ars Technica has a great tutorial on how to use a Leap Motion controller to play a classic side scrolling game. The user controls a space ship by moving their hand up and down (arstechnica.com/information-technology/2014/04/building-a-gesture-controlled-web-game-with-leap-motion/).

This game can be modified by changing the ending scene with a clue or code. The code is written in JavaScript, which is a common programming language with which many librarians are familiar. This makes modifying the code much easier than it would be in other programming languages.

PROJECT 7
Use "The Force" Maze

This is by far the coolest and most fun project of all listed. It incorporates robotics and puzzle solving. Plus, what escape room user wouldn't want to control a robot using just their hands? Leap Motion has a tutorial on how to control a Sphero robotic ball with the Leap Motion controller at gallery.leapmotion.com/leap-motion-sphero/. The controller allows a user to guide the robot with hand gestures.

For an escape room puzzle, you can create a giant-sized puzzle from wood or cardboard to create a classic box puzzle maze with a rolling marble. The user then must navigate the robot ball using hand gestures. The endpoint can either eject the ball or engage a mechanical trigger. To prevent cheating, enclose the maze in Plexiglass. If the tutorial seems too difficult, you can use a Sphero with a hand-gesture controller.

Bonus Projects

The following advanced projects are linked to how-to tutorials. Although they are a little more advanced, they can be built fairly easily. A description is given on how to use each for an escape room puzzle.

BONUS PROJECT 1

Rubik's Cube Solver

User matt2uy at instructables.com has created an Arduino project that will solve a Rubik's Cube. This project does not require expensive or special materials. In fact, you can create the solver with popsicle sticks and a few pieces of wood. The electronic components consist of an Arduino UNO R3, a couple of servos, and wires. Detailed instructions can be found at www.instructables.com/id/Rubiks-Cube-Solver/.

This project is a great way to introduce users to robotics and artificial intelligence. How can it be used as an escape room puzzle? Each solved side can have a number or word written on it that can be used to unlock a combination to solve a word puzzle.

Here is a simple example. You will need a lockbox with a combination or padlock, Rubik's Cube, and the Rubik's Cube solver. Write the combination numbers on a solved Rubik's Cube. Use one side for each number. Make sure to properly identify the sequence. For example, if the combination is 34-23-5 use "#1:34, #2: 23, #3:5" when labeling the cube. This will ensure there is no confusion in the sequence. Once you have the combination written on the cube, scramble up the cube and place it next to the solver. Create some simple instructions on how to load the cube and turn on the solver. A fun and visually pleasing trick is to use a giant switch or push button labeled "Push me now!" to start the machine.

BONUS PROJECT 2

Micro Servo Robot

User Pinaut at Let's Make Robots has created a mini robotic arm. This project does not require expensive or special materials. It is a small robotic arm that is controlled by mimicking movements. The electronic components consist of an Arduino, a couple of servos, a potentiometer, and wires. Detailed instructions can be found at https://www.robotshop.com/letsmakerobots/micro-servo-robot.

This project can be used like the classic arcade claw game. The robot can be placed behind an enclosure. The goal is for the user to simulate the movement that grabs an object and rolls it down a chute. The object can contain a code that unlocks a combination lock or a word that is part of a bigger puzzle.

•••••••

Jennifer Thoegersen, data curation librarian at the University of Nebraska-Lincoln offers this walkthrough tutorial for how to create an exciting robot maze for an escape room game.

How to Build a Robot Maze

As part of the escape room I helped build along with Rasmus Thoegersen (now at the Museum of Danish America) at Morton-James Public Library in Nebraska City, we worked with a group of children to create a robot maze. Here is the basic how-to for our maze.

Supplies List

- Dash & Dot
- tablet with Bluetooth
- 8' × 4' particle board
- 40' of ¾" boards
- 8.5' × 4.5' clear vinyl
- wood glue
- *Optional:* spray paint

Tools List

- chalk line
- tape measure
- markers
- stapler
- scissors
- table saw

Program the Robots

Dash and Dot are programmable robots made by Wonder Workshop. Download the Blockly for Dash & Dot Robots app (available for Android and Apple). Using this app, you can program the robots to do a variety of things using the Blockly programming language. Connect the robots to the app and create a program with the following blocks:

- When Dot Top Button → Forward 40 normal
- When Dot Button 3 → Backward 40 normal
- When Dot Button 2 → Turn Left 30 degrees
- When Dot Button 1 → Turn Right 30 degrees
- When Dash Top Button → My Sounds #1 (Clearly record yourself saying the lock combination)

With this program, a player can push the buttons on the top of the Dot robot to navigate Dash out of the maze. After retrieving Dash from the maze, the player would press Dash's middle button to play a recording of the lock combination.

Design the Maze

- On a piece of paper, create a 9 × 4 grid and sketch out where the walls of the maze will be.
- On the particle board, use a chalk line to create lines along the board at the points.
- Using your sketch as a guide, color in where the walls should be with a marker.
- Make a list of the lengths of the wall segments, remembering to include the outer walls.
- Cut boards to length and glue them in place using wood glue.
- *Optional:* Paint the interior of the maze.
- Stretch the clear vinyl over the top of the maze and staple it into place. Do not staple down the corner closest to Dash's starting point, so you are able to slip him into place without navigating him through the whole maze.

Playing the Maze

When preparing your escape room to be played, turn the robots on, connect them to the Blockly app, and start the Blockly program. Get Dash into starting position, place Dot somewhere visible in the room, and place the tablet where players can't get to it.

Players will press the buttons on Dot to navigate Dash out of the maze. Once they get him out, they must press his top button to hear the lock combination.

Remember to turn off and charge Dash, Dot, and the tablet between groups playing the room.

Revamp

The maze concept can be revamped in many ways to make it easier and cheaper. For example, a remote-control car can be used instead of Dash and Dot.

• • • • • • •

NOTE

1. Claire Reilly, "Inside the Enigma: The Tech behind an Escape Room," *CNet Culture,* March 12, 2015, https://www.cnet.com/news/inside-the-enigma-room-the-technology-behind-an-escape-room/.

14

Start-to-Finish Model

The Search for Alexander Hamilton and the Missing Librarian: A Time Travel Adventure

THERE ARE PLENTY OF FREE ESCAPE ROOMS AVAILABLE ONLINE for you to download and host, as you read about in chapter 3. In addition, here is a walkthrough of the game that I designed, *The Search for Alexander Hamilton and the Missing Librarian: A Time Travel Adventure*. By the end of this walkthrough you should have all you need to get started hosting this room in your own library.

THE SEARCH FOR ALEXANDER HAMILTON AND THE MISSING LIBRARIAN

A Time Travel Adventure

The premise for this escape room game is that there is an active crime scene that investigators need to examine to find the clues to determine the whereabouts of the missing librarian. Investigators have 30 minutes before the crime scene is cleared or the mystery of what happened to Addison Adley will go unsolved. Here is the introduction:

> Resident librarian, cat lover, and conspiracy theorist Addison Adley has vanished into thin air. She was last seen in the private library of Alexander Hamilton conducting research surrounding her life's work and obsession, which was her theory that founding father Alexander Hamilton did not die on July 12, 1804 as a result of his duel with Aaron Burr, but instead was actually an intrepid

> time traveler who used the incident as an opportunity to disappear to travel through the ages. Not surprisingly, the authorities are not taking this seriously. Your job is to find clues as to her disappearance before the local police come in to clear the crime scene and disrupt everything. You have thirty minutes. Your best bet is to start with the staff witness statements.

The game includes a locked iPad along with six locked boxes, one of which is a wooden box utilizing a magnetic lock for the final puzzle of the game. The puzzles include both linear and nonlinear challenges to engage players and vary from word puzzles to hidden items to ciphers. The locks are mainly those included in the Breakout EDU lock kit. This escape room is meant to take place in a library setting (see figure 14.1), but the game is designed to be mobile, so it can easily be set up anywhere.

The game begins with the host reading the Introduction to players before they go into the room in order to get them engrossed in the narrative from the outset. As players enter the room, they see three main "stations" with objects, along with decorations and crime scene tape delimiting the play area. The first station is an investigator's table that has the final locked wooden box on it, along with the witness statements and a chalkboard, some chalk, and an

FIGURE 14.1
Alexander Hamilton Escape Room set-up

eraser for players to use during the game (see figure 14.2). The next station is the missing librarian, Addison Adley's library carrel where she conducted her research. And the last station is a nearby bookshelf or desk with even more clues strewn about.

The game starts out with three nonlinear puzzles at the beginning of the game, which players can tackle at the same time. In the narrative introduction, investigators have been pointed toward the staff witness statements, so this is likely where they will begin. As they read over these statements they will notice the word *nuts* is repeatedly used. The statement of one librarian claims that she smelled roasting chestnuts around the time that Addison disappeared, while another mentions that she always brought in homemade hazelnut coffee. Two of the librarians comment about her nutty ramblings and the fact that she seemed a little nuts. These clues point the way to a bowl of imitation walnuts (used to prevent issues with people who have nut allergies), with the iPad lock combination written on individual nuts. I chose to include a magnifying glass as one of the props in this area for those people who may need help reading the small numbers written on the nuts, but that is optional. Once investigators unlock the iPad, they see that the sole item is a video diary entry of Addison ranting about how she knows that everyone thinks she's crazy, but that everyone will find out the truth in the end. In the video she offers two clues, one for the final puzzle of the game—"Pink is last"—and one for the four-digit lockbox puzzle—"the soldier's number is seven."

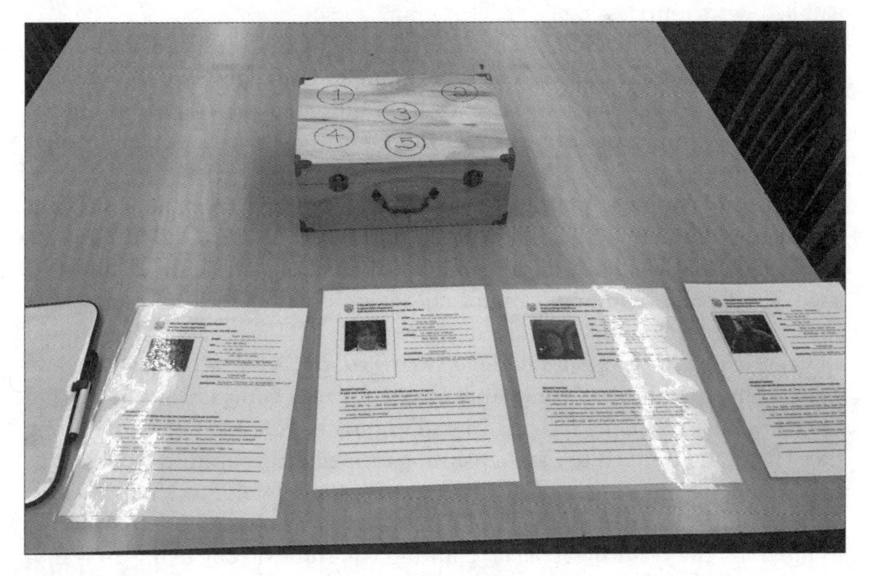

FIGURE 14.2
Investigator's table

Also found in Addison's carrel (figure 14.3) is her purse, which contains a few items including a $10 bill (the note on which Alexander Hamilton appears) with all but the first three serial numbers blacked out with marker. This second nonlinear puzzle can be solved right away when investigators find the $10 bill. This can be used to unlock the three-digit locked box. Within that locked box, players will find another four-digit lockbox clue as well as Addison's handwritten journal. Players must hold on to the second four-digit lock clue until later in the game, but the journal can be read and used right away. The journal is filled with entries rambling about Alexander Hamilton's time-traveling adventures, and a call number scribbled in red ink in the margin of one of the pages. The call number leads players to a book in a bookshelf within the gameplay area of the library. It holds a postcard image of Alexander Hamilton's grave with a third four-digit lockbox clue.

FIGURE 14.3
Addison Adley's library carrel

The third nonlinear puzzle that can be tackled right away is the signal flags of the ships of war puzzle. I designed this puzzle because I wanted to integrate a challenge that used a form of communication from Alexander Hamilton's time. The form of communication I chose was one in which messages were sent via flags flown on ships during times of war. These signal flags would let other ships in the fleet or armada know exactly what action to take and could even communicate commands in the form of compass directions. On the University of Rhode Island's Digital Commons, I found a book decoding these flags and decided to have a painting created incorporating certain flags that would give investigators clues for the directional/color lock in the game. Luckily, I have an artist in the family (my Mom!), who was more than happy to pitch in. The resulting *Armada* painting has ships of war flying a total of three flags that when decoded indicate four compass directions and the color yellow, which is the combination needed for the directional/color lock. Once

FIGURE 14.4
Librarians solving the mystery

this box is opened, players receive the last four-digit lockbox clue along with a cat statue with an orange good-luck charm and a transparent overlay that fits atop the half-finished crossword puzzle on Addison's desk. Figure 14.4 shows the librarian-players "at work." When investigators place the overlay on top of the crossword puzzle, they can see the five circled letters that they need to unscramble to spell the word *RIVAL*. This word unlocks a five-digit alphabet locked box that contains a cat statue with a yellow good luck charm and a Polaroid photo of another cat statue with an orange charm on the locked wooden box in a particular place. There are five numbers on the wooden box and players must place all the cat statues in their proper order to unlock the box.

At this point investigators have all four clues to the 4-digit lockbox and can now open it. Within that box is a green-charmed cat statue, a Polaroid of two more cat statues—with blue and yellow charms—in their proper places on the final cat box puzzle, and a UV flashlight along with a scroll that says, "may the light of your will guide me." As of this time, investigators should have all but the last (pink-charmed) cat statue as the remaining statue—blue—can be found hidden in plain sight around the clue stations within the gameplay room. They should also know the order of each cat statue as they have received clues for the placement of each in the various puzzles. In the "She's Nuts" puzzle they got the clue that pink is last, the crossword puzzle revealed that orange is first (in the Polaroid), the four-digit lockbox puzzle indicated that blue and yellow cats are placed third and fourth. This leaves only the second space open for the green-charmed cat.

The UV flashlight and the scroll should lead investigators to wave the light over Alexander Hamilton's last will and testament, which is on the nearby desk. Written in UV ink is the message "the librarian holds the key." The librarian host will then give the players the key to the keyed lock box containing the final pink cat statue. I chose to do this because I wanted to make sure that the final cat statue was not found until the very end of the game. I used a child-proof magnetic cabinet lock on the final locked wooden box, and the magnet was glued inside of the pink cat statue which served as the key to unlocking the box. Once investigators place the final pink cat statue on the number 5 circle on the box, the magnetic lock will unlock and the box can be opened. Inside the box is a postcard from the future from the missing librarian Addison Adley and Alexander Hamilton himself with the following text:

> To: 21st Century Doubters, Greetings from the year 3105! Alex and I are having a blast. The world is grand, and print still isn't dead! All the best, Addison

This ends the game.

To supplement this descriptive walkthrough of the game, I have created detailed documents indicating how to set up the room as well as detailing how each puzzle works. These are both included below. You can also find the puzzle flowchart in chapter 5. And here is a video overview of entire game set-up in two parts:

Part 1: https://www.dropbox.com/s/n58ztp85zrtjy33/Hamilton_Rooom_Walkthru.mp4?dl=0 *or* http://bit.ly/2GrTA02
Part 2: https://www.dropbox.com/s/bg1i04q69qpnlug/Hamilton_Room_Walkthru2.mp4?dl=0 *or* http://bit.ly/2DqOEwK

All the props and items used in the game are easily found. I also provide access to the digital files such as an image of the *Armada* painting, staff witness statements, Addison's video entry, and so on, for those items I created. You're free to use them. In the next section I go into detail about where to purchase, where to download, and how to make each prop.

HOW TO MAKE/WHERE TO BUY THE PROPS

You will notice that the set-up document in this chapter has a complete list of assets and props needed to run this game. Here is how you find and/or make them.

Documents and Digital Files I Included in the Game (Dropbox folder at https://www.dropbox.com/sh/5t5uec4rw4uiw2a/AAC6jUku7VuXPxi-lbjgBa-Ma?dl=0 *or* http://bit.ly/2Ii4E7P):

- Staff witness statements
- Addison Adley's video entry
- Image of Alexander Hamilton's grave
- *Armada* painting (can be printed out as a poster at Kinkos)
- Images of Addison's handwritten journal
- Images of the Polaroids that can be printed
- Postcard from the future from Addison and Alexander Hamilton
- Victory sign

Other documents and digital files available online include:

A Collection of the Facts and Documents, Relative to the Death of Major-General Alexander Hamilton. The full book can be bought on Amazon but may also be freely downloaded for printing from https://archive.org/details/collectionoffact00cole.

Good luck cat statues: free 3-D printable files are available at https://www.thingiverse.com/thing:1328335.

The Founding Fathers crossword puzzle can be downloaded for $1 from https://www.teacherspayteachers.com/Product/Founding-Fathers-Crossword-Puzzle-Version-1–1030997.

"*Signal Book for Ships of War*" can be downloaded at no charge from http://digitalcommons.uri.edu/cgi/viewcontent.cgi?article=1018&context=sc_pubs. I had this printed on parchment paper and bound at Kinkos for the game.

Alexander Hamilton's will is in *A Collection of the Facts and Documents, Relative to the Death of Major-General Alexander Hamilton* and is also available for free download at https://founders.archives.gov/documents/Hamilton/01-26-02-0001-0259.

Other Props:

- Yellow crime scene tape—Lowe's or Home Depot
- Chalkboard, chalk, eraser—Dollar Tree
- Three mini lockable toolboxes—Dollar Tree
- Two Breakout.edu lock boxes—Breakout EDU
- Locks—Breakout EDU or Amazon
- UV ink and flashlight—Breakout EDU or Amazon
- iPad—you may want to borrow one of these as I did
- Sheet of clear plastic to draw crossword puzzle overlay boxes—Dollar Tree or craft store

- Bowl of fake walnuts—Michael's or AC Moore craft stores
- Magnifying glass—Dollar Tree
- Addison's purse—you could borrow one of these as I did
- Alexander Hamilton bookmarks—You can make your own or purchase these at https://www.etsy.com/listing/490307107/alexander-hamilton-hamilton-bookmark
- Wall clock—you can set your wall clock to 4:00 or you can simply change that clue to read "lawyer=4" instead
- Hidden book—choose a library book on a bookshelf within the gameplay area and hide the postcard image in it. Don't forget to write the call number in the margin of the journal
- Magnetic wooden lock box—you can use a hinged wooden box from Michael's or AC Moore craft stores. The locking mechanism can be made with a child-safety lock that is typically used on cabinets. The large key with the magnet in it can be dissolved in acetone leaving only the magnet if the key is too big to glue inside your cats. Numbered spots on the top of the box can be wood-burned or drawn with a marker.

ESCAPE ROOM SET-UP DOCUMENT

The Search for Alexander Hamilton and the Missing Librarian
A Time Travel Adventure

Introduction

This is the narrative introduction that is to be read to players before entering the room.

> Resident librarian, cat lover, and conspiracy theorist Addison Adley has vanished into thin air. She was last seen in the private library of Alexander Hamilton conducting research surrounding her life's work and obsession, which was her theory that founding father Alexander Hamilton did not die on July 12, 1804, as a result of his duel with Aaron Burr, but instead was actually an intrepid time traveler who used the incident as an opportunity to disappear to travel through

the ages. Not surprisingly, the authorities are not taking this seriously. Your job is to find clues as to her disappearance before the local police come in to clear the crime scene and disrupt everything. You have thirty minutes. Your best bet is to start with the staff witness statements.

Some brief information about the game:

- Please stay within the crime scene tape.
- Please don't attempt to take apart anything within the room.
- You have 30 minutes to solve the room.
- You may ask for clues/hints as you play the game—there are two hint cards hidden in the gameplay area.
- Some of the locks are upside down on the boxes, I have placed a white mark indicating on which side you'll start entering the lock combination.
- Communication with your fellow teammates is key to solving this room.

Assets and Props

These are all the items that will be needed to host this game.

- Yellow crime scene tape
- Chalkboard, chalk, and eraser
- Laminated staff witness statements
- Five locked boxes
- Locks
    - Alphabet lock
    - Directional/color lock
    - Key lock
    - Three-digit number lock
    - Four-digit number lock
- One wooden magnetic lock box
- One iPad with Addison's video entry
- Bowl of fake walnuts with number clues to unlock iPad
- Magnifying glass
- Five good luck cat statues—one (blue) hidden around library, four in locked boxes

- Three postcard images of Alexander Hamilton's grave, each with a four-digit lock clue written on it
- Addison's purse, filled with:
  - A $10 bill with all but the first three serial numbers blacked out
  - Reading glasses
  - Tissues
  - Lipstick
  - Mirror
  - UV pen (in case you need to rewrite any clues)
- A row of Alexander Hamilton-related library books
- The book *A Collection of the Facts and Documents, Relative to the Death of Major-General Alexander Hamilton*
- Unfinished crossword puzzle
- Transparent overlay for crossword puzzle
- Addison's hand-written journal
- Alexander Hamilton bookmarks
- *Armada* painting
- Wall clock set to 4:00
- Hidden book with four-digit lock clue postcard in it.
- Book: "*Signal Book for Ships of War*"
- Two hint cards
- Postcard from the future from Addison and Alexander Hamilton

Set-Up List

This is how the room is set up, where everything goes, and how to stock and restock the locked boxes and set the lock combinations.

On Investigation Table

- Staff witness statements
- Chalkboard and chalk/eraser for investigators
- One wooden magnetic box (final puzzle)

Throughout the Room

- Five locked boxes: 3 mini toolboxes, 1 large Breakout EDU box, 1 small Breakout EDU box

In Addison Adley's Library Carrel

- Bowl of walnuts
- Locked iPad
- Addison's purse
- A row of Alexander Hamilton- related library books.
- The book *A Collection of the Facts and Documents, Relative to the Death of Major-General Alexander Hamilton*
- Unfinished crossword puzzle
- Other books, envelopes, red herrings

On the Walls

- *Armada* painting
- Wall clock set to 4:00

On Bookshelf/Table Nearby

- Hidden book with four-digit lock clue in it
- The book *Signal Book for Ships of War*
- Alexander Hamilton's will
- Blue cat statue

Other Areas

- Set up crime scene tape to limit play in "crime scene" gameplay area.
- Set up soundtrack on Tabletop Audio (https://tabletopaudio.com) to loop and continuously play during gameplay—playlist contains these three songs: "Noir Procedural," "Super Hero," and "Waiting Time."
- Set up timer (http://facilitationtool.BreakoutEDU.com/index.php?key=mh8fsaD1sNBAokM).

Locked and Hidden Items to Set Up

Locked/Hidden Item	Lock Type	Combination	Contents
iPad	Four-digit password	5 9 7 3	Video containing a four-digit lockbox puzzle clue—The soldier's number is 7, and final cat box puzzle clue—pink is last
Mini toolbox	Three-digit combination lock	8 4 2	A photo of Hamilton's grave with a four-digit lockbox puzzle clue—statesman=2, Addison's handwritten journal with call number scribbled in margin
Mini toolbox	Five-digit directional/color lock	SE NE Yellow (down, right, up, right, yellow)	A photo of Hamilton's grave with a four-digit lockbox puzzle clue—man=8, crossword puzzle overlay, orange cat statue
Hidden book	Choose a library book on a nearby bookshelf within the gameplay area. Write that call number in journal.		A photo of Hamilton's grave with a four-digit lockbox puzzle clue—the lawyer watches the clock
Large Breakout EDU lock box	Four-digit combo lock	7 2 4 8	Green cat statue, UV/black-light flashlight, scroll saying "may the light of your will guide me," Polaroid with blue and yellow cat statues in their proper order (spots 3 and 4) on final cat box puzzle
Mini toolbox	Five-digit alphabet lock	R I V A L	The yellow cat statue, Polaroid of orange cat statue in its proper order (spot #1) on final cat box puzzle
Small Breakout EDU lock box	Key lock	Key	The pink cat statue
Wooden box with magnetic lock	Cats in proper order 1-orange, 2-green, 3-blue, 4-yellow, 5-pink		Postcard from the future from Addison and Alexander Hamilton

ESCAPE ROOM PUZZLE DOCUMENT

The Search for Alexander Hamilton and the Missing Librarian

A Time Travel Adventure

This is a detailed document of every puzzle within *The Search for Alexander Hamilton and the Missing Librarian: A Time Travel Adventure* escape room game and how they work.

PUZZLE NAME
"She's Nuts"

Puzzle Type:	Open
Puzzle Prerequisites:	None
Pointer Clues:	Staff witness statements, bowl of walnuts in Addison's carrel
Locked Item:	iPad
Lock Combo:	5 9 7 3
Treasure/Contents:	Video containing a four-digit lockbox puzzle clue (the soldier's number is 7), final cat box puzzle clue (pink is last)
Description:	Players will notice that in the staff witness statements, each librarian mentions that Addison is a little crazy or nutty. They will see a locked iPad with an "I heart Alex" sticker on it, and a bowl of walnuts in her carrel along with a magnifying glass. Upon further inspection of the nuts, players will notice small numbers written on four of the nuts with dashes indicating the order of the numbers in the combination; 5, _9, _ _7, _ _ _3 to unlock the iPad. Once unlocked, the sole item on the iPad is a video of Addison ranting about how everyone will see that she's not nuts in the end. She gives a clue to two puzzles in her video entry—one for the four-digit lockbox puzzle (the soldier's number is 7) and one for the final cat box puzzle (pink is last).

PUZZLE NAME

$10 Bill

Puzzle Type:	Open
Puzzle Prerequisites:	None
Pointer Clues:	Librarian's purse with $10 bill
Locked Item:	Mini toolbox with three-digit combination lock
Lock Combo:	8 4 2
Treasure/Contents:	A photo of Alexander Hamilton's grave with a four-digit lockbox puzzle (clue—statesman=2), Addison's handwritten journal with call number scribbled in margin.
Description:	There are very few items in Addison's purse, one of which is a $10 with all but the first three numbers of the serial number blacked out with marker. These numbers are the combination to the three-digit combo lock. That box contains another clue for the four-digit lockbox puzzle (statesman=2), along with Addison's handwritten journal of her rantings about Alexander Hamilton's time travels. On one of the pages, there is a call number scribbled in red ink in the margin leading to the hidden book puzzle.

PUZZLE NAME

Hidden Book

Puzzle Type:	Linear
Puzzle Prerequisites:	$10 Bill
Pointer Clues:	Addison Adley's journal with call number leading to book
Locked Item:	none
Lock Combo:	none
Treasure/Contents:	A photo of Alexander Hamilton's grave with a four-digit lockbox puzzle clue–the lawyer watches the clock (broken clock on the wall reads 4:00)
Description:	Within the $10 bill puzzle lock box is Addison's handwritten journal with her rantings about Alexander Hamilton's time travel adventures. On one of the pages of that journal is a call number written in red ink in one of the margins that leads

players to this book. The book has a photo of Hamilton's grave with a four-digit lockbox puzzle clue in it (the lawyer watches the clock) which leads players to look at the broken clock on the wall that reads 4:00. This gives them the number 4 to add to the clues for the four-digit lockbox puzzle.

PUZZLE NAME

Signal Flags of Ships of War

Puzzle Type: Open

Puzzle Prerequisites: None

Pointer Clues: Painting on the wall with signal flags on an armada, book *Signal Book for Ships of War*

Locked Item: Mini toolbox with five-digit directional/color lock

Lock Combo: SE NE yellow (down, right, up, right, yellow)

Treasure/Contents: A photo of Hamilton's grave with a four-digit lockbox puzzle clue (man=8,) crossword puzzle overlay, orange cat statue

Description: Players will find the book *Signal Book for Ships of War* on one of the nearby bookshelves. Within that book is a code for how to communicate with other ships during wartime by using certain flags. The painting on the wall depicts three ships, each with a different flag. Players will look up those flags in the book to determine that they indicate compass directions SE, NE, and the color yellow for fire. They will use that information to open the directional/color lock on one of the mini toolboxes. The box contains one of the four-digit lockbox puzzle clues (man=8), and an overlay that can be placed on the half-finished crossword puzzle in Addison's carrel, along with the orange-charmed cat statue.

PUZZLE NAME

Crossword Puzzle

Puzzle Type: Linear

Puzzle Prerequisites: Signal Flags of Ships of War

Pointer Clues: Founding Fathers half-finished crossword puzzle on Addison's carrel, crossword puzzle overlay with letters circled that when unscrambled spell RIVAL

Locked Item: Mini toolbox with five-digit alphabet lock

Lock Combo: R I V A L

Treasure/Contents: The yellow cat statue, Polaroid of the orange cat statue in its proper order (first) on final cat box puzzle.

Description: Addison's carrel has an unfinished "Founding Fathers" crossword puzzle in it. Once players solve the signal flags of ships of war puzzle they receive an overlay for that puzzle, which circles five letters within that puzzle. When unscrambled they spell out the word RIVAL which is the combination for the alphabet lock. Once the mini toolbox is opened, players receive the yellow cat statue along with a Polaroid of the orange cat statue in its proper order (first) for the final cat box puzzle box. Once this puzzle is solved, players will know that the orange cat statue goes first, the blue and yellow are third and fourth (from the four-digit lockbox puzzle), and the pink statue is last (from the "She's Nuts" puzzle). Players will need to deduce that the green cat statue goes second.

PUZZLE NAME
Four-Digit Lockbox

Puzzle Type: Linear

Puzzle Prerequisites: "She's Nuts," Signal Flags of Ships of War, $10 Bill, Hidden Book

Pointer Clues: Addison's video on the iPad, three postcard photos of Alexander Hamilton's grave with numbers to the lock, book in Addison's carrel—*A Collection of the Facts and Documents, Relative to the Death of Major-General Alexander Hamilton* with his obituary in the *Daily Advertiser* giving the order of numbers for the four-digit lock.

Locked Item: Large Breakout EDU lock box with four-digit combo lock

Lock Combo: 7 2 4 8

Treasure/Contents: UV or black-light flashlight, scroll saying "may the light of your will guide me," Polaroid with blue and yellow cat statues in their proper order (places 3 and 4) in final cat box puzzle, the green cat statue.

Description: The book in Addison's carrel, *A Collection of the Facts and Documents, Relative to the Death of Major-General Alexander Hamilton,* contains an obituary in the *Daily Advertiser* that discusses Hamilton as a soldier, a statesman, a lawyer, and a man, in that order. Those aspects are highlighted in the book and that page is bookmarked, giving players the information needed to decipher the order of the clues that are found written on three postcard images of his grave within the lock boxes of puzzles: signal flags of ships of war, $10 bill, and hidden book along with Addison's video within the "She's Nuts" puzzle. This lock box contains the green cat statue, a UV black light flashlight, and a scroll that reads "may the light of your will guide me," which will lead players to Hamilton's will. It also contains a Polaroid of the blue and yellow cat statues in their proper order on final cat box puzzle box.

PUZZLE NAME
Hamilton's Will

Puzzle Type: Linear

Puzzle Prerequisites: Four-digit lockbox

Pointer Clues: Alexander Hamilton's will, UV flashlight, scroll with "may the light of your will guide me" written on it

Locked Item: Small Breakout EDU lock box with key lock

Lock Combo: Key

Treasure/Contents: The pink cat statue

Description: After solving the four-digit lockbox puzzle, players are given a UV flashlight along with a scroll reading "may the light of your will guide me." When they shine the flashlight over Alexander Hamilton's will, they will see the words "the librarian holds the key" revealing the location of the key to the lockbox with the key lock. Players will then be given the key by their librarian host. Within that small Breakout EDU lock box is the final pink cat statue for the final cat box puzzle.

PUZZLE NAME
Final Cat Box Puzzle

Puzzle Type:	Linear
Puzzle Prerequisites:	"She's Nuts," Four-Digit Lockbox, Crossword Puzzle, Hamilton's Will
Pointer Clues:	Cat statues (four in locked boxes, one hidden around library), Polaroids of cat statues
Locked Item:	Wooden box with magnetic lock
Lock Combo:	Cats in proper order 1—orange, 2—green, 3—blue, 4—yellow, 5—pink
Treasure/Contents:	Postcard from the future from Addison and Alexander Hamilton.
Description:	Once players solve the Hamilton's Will puzzle and find the final good luck cat (pink), they can open the final magnetic box. They should now know the order of the cats from the "She's Nuts" puzzle (pink is last), the crossword puzzle (orange is first), the four-digit Lockbox puzzle (blue and yellow are third and fourth), and with no other place open for it that leaves green as second.

This is the complete documentation to prepare for, set up, and run this escape room game. Blank templates for both documents can be found in appendixes 1 and 2 if you are creating your own game. Hopefully these eleven escape room projects included in this and previous chapters will inspire you to start hosting these exciting and incredibly customizable games yourself!

APPENDIX A

Escape Room Set-up Document Template

Escape Room Title:____

Introduction

This is the narrative introduction that is to be read to players before entering the room.

[*Insert your narrative's introductory paragraph here*]

Some brief information about the game:

- Please stay within the gameplay.
- Please don't attempt to take apart anything within the room.
- You have 60 minutes to solve the room.
- You may ask for three clues or hints as you play the game.
- Communication with your fellow teammates is key to solving this room.

Assets and Props

These are *all* the items that will be needed to host this game.

[*List every item, lockbox, lock, prop, decoration, and red herring here.*]

Available to download on Dropbox here: http://bit.ly/2FJs9VH

Set-Up List

This is how the room is set up, where everything goes, and how to stock and restock the locked boxes and set the lock combinations.

Station/Area 1:

Station/Area 2:

Station/Area 3:

Station/Area 4:

On the walls:

Miscellaneous:

Soundtrack?

Set up timer

(http://facilitationtool.BreakoutEDU.com/index.php?key=mh8fsaD1sNBAokM)

Locked and hidden items to set up:

Locked/Hidden Item	*Lock Type*	*Combination*	*Contents*

APPENDIX B

Escape Room Puzzle Document Template

Escape Room Title:____

This is a detailed document of every puzzle within the ____________________ escape room.

Puzzle 1 Name:

Puzzle type: Linear or nonlinear

Puzzle Prerequisites:

Pointer Clues:

Locked Item:

Lock Combo:

Treasure/Contents:

Description:

Puzzle 2 Name:

Puzzle Type: Linear or nonlinear

Puzzle Prerequisites:

Pointer Clues:

Locked Item:

Lock Combo:

Treasure/Contents:

Description:

Available to download on Dropbox here: http://bit.ly/2ItD7R8

Puzzle 3 Name:

Puzzle Type: Linear or nonlinear

Puzzle Prerequisites:

Pointer Clues:

Locked Item:

Lock Combo:

Treasure/Contents:

Description:

Puzzle 4 Name:

Puzzle Type: Linear or nonlinear

Puzzle Prerequisites:

Pointer Clues:

Locked Item:

Lock Combo:

Treasure/Contents:

Description:

Puzzle 5 Name:

Puzzle Type: Linear or nonlinear

Puzzle Prerequisites:

Pointer Clues:

Locked Item:

Lock Combo:

Treasure/Contents:

Description:

Puzzle 6 Name:

Puzzle Type: Linear or nonlinear

Puzzle Prerequisites:

Pointer Clues:

Locked Item:

Lock Combo:

Treasure/Contents:

Description:

Puzzle 7 Name:

Puzzle Type: Linear or nonlinear

Puzzle Prerequisites:

Pointer Clues:

Locked Item:

Lock Combo:

Treasure/Contents:

Description:

Resources

Directories

Escaping Guru
    https://escapinguru.com

Escape Rooms Directory (No longer being updated but is a source of thousands of escape rooms)
    http://escaperoomdirectory.com

International Association of Escape Games (over 3,500 games listed)
    www.iaescapegames.com

LARP List Worldwide directory of LARPs
    www.larping.org/larps

Play Exit Games: The World's Largest Escape Room Directory
    www.playexitgames.com

USA Escape Rooms Directory
    https://usaescaperooms.com

Educational Resources

Breakout EDU: Educational immersive learning games platform
    https://www.BreakoutEDU.com

Lock Paper Scissors: Escape Games: The Boredom-Crushing Classroom Tech Your Students Need.
    https://lockpaperscissors.co/school-escape-games

Forums and Community Groups

Escape Rooms Subreddit Community
https://www.reddit.com/r/escaperooms

Facebook Groups
Breakout EDU
https://www.facebook.com/groups/Breakout EDU
Escape Room Enthusiasts
https://www.facebook.com/groups/escaperoomenthusiasts
Escape Room Technology and Props
https://www.facebook.com/groups/1245590885468531
League of Librarian Gamers—ALA RT
https://www.facebook.com/groups/LeagueOfLibrarianGamers
Library Escape Room Enthusiasts
https://www.facebook.com/groups/1922174474731812
Library Teachers (Breakout EDU)
https://www.facebook.com/groups/Breakout EDUlibrary

Other groups for the following areas of education:

Art and Music Teachers (Breakout EDU)
Elementary Teachers (Breakout EDU)
English Teachers (Breakout EDU)
Gifted and Talented Program Teachers (Breakout EDU)
History Teachers (Breakout EDU)
Math Teachers (Breakout EDU)
Science Teachers (Breakout EDU)
Spanish Teachers (Breakout EDU)

Blogs

Esc Room Addict is an organization of more than 40 escape room specialists and reviewers who share their insights.
http://escroomaddict.com

Escape Authority is a blog written by Chris Moschella, who has played over 300 escape room games in the US.[1]
https://escapeauthority.com

Escape Room Tips offers posts from William Chen and Yuan Jiang, who have played 150 escape room games together.
http://escroomaddict.com

Intervirals is a blog written by an Australian escape rooms enthusiast.
https://intervirals.wordpress.com

Now Escape is both a directory platform and a blog with helpful advice about designing escape rooms.
http://blog.nowescape.com

Room Escape Artist is penned by escape room enthusiasts Lisa and David Spira, who have played more than 450 escape room games throughout the world.
https://roomescapeartist.com

Books

Breaking into Breakout Boxes: Escape Rooms in Education, Holly Elizabeth Johnson (July 22, 2017: CreateSpace Independent Publishing Platform).

Escape Room Rules—How to Create an Amazing Game, Kindle book (July 16, 2016: Ever NowCo).

Escape the Game: How to Make Puzzles and Escape Rooms, Adam Clare and Samet Choudhury (August 3, 2016: CreateSpace Independent Publishing Platform).

Paper Escapes: A Fun and Exciting ESCAPE ROOM Experience at Home, Volume 1, Jesse Cruz (April 8, 2017: CreateSpace Independent Publishing Platform).

Presentations

"Do(n't) Panic! A Manual for Original Library Escape Room Events." Nicole Scherer, head of teen services at Connecticut's Fairfield Public Library, put together an entire manual on how to develop original escape rooms. This guide is jam-packed with tips for creating your own escape games in your library.
http://bit.ly/2If9ti7

Presentation on Breakout EDU Digital. French teacher Sylvia Duckworth gave this presentation at Google for Education's Irvine Custom Summit on Breakout EDU Digital, January 28–29, 2017.
http:// bit.ly/ 2txreGu

Articles

"Breakout EDU Brings 'Escape Room' Strategy to the Classroom. SLJ Review," Phil Goerner, *School Library Journal,* September 7, 2016, https://www.slj.com/2016/09/reviews/tech/breakout-edu-brings-escape-room-strategy-to-the-classroom-slj-review/.

"'Breakout' of the Mold: Breakout Programs in Libraries," Kate Lewallen, *Programming Librarian.* May 17, 2017, www.programminglibrarian.org/blog/breakout-mold-breakout-programs-libraries.

"Libraries on Lockdown: Escape Rooms, A Breakout Trend in Youth Programming," Katie O'Reilly, *American Libraries,* September 1, 2016, https://americanlibrariesmagazine.org/2016/09/01/escape-rooms-libraries-on-lockdown/.

"Library Escape Rooms: Keeping Your Patrons Captive," Derek Murphy, *Unbound*, April 4, 2014, http://slis.simmons.edu/blogs/unbound/2016/04/14/library-escape-rooms.

"TPiB: Locked in the Library! Hosting an Escape Room Program at Your Library School," Heather Booth, *Library Journal,* July 14, 2016, www.teenlibrariantoolbox.com/2016/07/tpib-locked-in-the-library/.

ARTWORK

If you're looking for artwork to use in your escape rooms, there's plenty to be found on Pinterest and Google Images. Or you can hire an affordable artist who will take on custom commissions for under $200 such as Penny Page, who painted the *Armadas* painting for my escape room.

Another resource is 16 Printable Treasure Maps Templates (https://lockpaperscissors.co/treasure-map-templates-2).[2]

NOTES

1. "10 Best Escape Rooms Readers' Choice Awards 2017," *USA Today,* www.10best.com/awards/travel/best-escape-room-2017/.
2. (Shameless plug for my Mom, who's awesome!) Penny Page is available to do custom paintings for escape rooms. She can be reached at penelopewood12@gmail.com, https://www.facebook.com/Pennys-Art-377126272429356/, or http://bit.ly/2FWD2qG.

INDEX

f denotes figures

#
5 Wits, 10
60OUT Escape Rooms, 10

A
The Abandoned Cabin, 137–138
Adley, Addison, 73–74, 155–156, 157, 158*f,* 160, 162–163
advocacy, 27–29
American Association of School Librarians (AASL), 36
American Libraries magazine, 3
American Museum of Natural History, 15
Arduino boards, 82, 106, 145, 146–147, 149–151
Armada (Page), 78*f,* 158, 160–161, 164–165, 182
articles, recommended, 181–182
artwork, resources for, 182
augmented reality (AR), 15–16, 114
AVATAR: Discover Pandora, 17

B
Bare Conductive Touch Board, 113, 146, 148
Bennett, Rozanna, 46–47
black-light puzzles, 60, 64, 69, 79, 171
blogs, list of, 180–181
board games, 65, 133–138
boffers, 118
bookmarks, 162
books, recommended, 181
Breakout EDU
 overview, 23–24, 33n1, 60n2, 63–64
 digital breakouts from, 125, 132
 examples of games by, 57–59, 94–102, 141
 lock kits from, 30, 40, 64, 69, 99, 166
 resource list on, 179–181
 as starting point, 42, 64, 69
Breakout KC, 11
Breakout! program, 41–42
Bucci, Marissa, 54–57
Bucks County (PA) Library System, 133
budgets and funding, 30–33, 108–109
Burton, Laura, 44–45

C

California escape rooms, 5, 10, 11, 12
capacitive touch, 148
cat puzzle, in Hamilton room, 76, 82*f*, 107*f*, 159–161, 170–172
Cerro Gordo School District, 45
Charlotte Mecklenburg Library, 51–52
children
  escape rooms designed by, 38–39
  escape rooms for, 38–39, 49–50, 119–124
Chinese good luck cat puzzle, 76, 82*f*, 107*f*, 159–161, 170–172
cinematic experiences, x, 17–20, 59, 112
circuit building, 147–148
Claustrophobia (Berlin), 6, 13
Cleveland Museum of Art, 15
A Clock Is Ticking program, 52–53
clubs, for enthusiasts, 103–109
Clue Carré, 11
ClueQuest, 12
clues
  creating, 74–75, 96–98
  in the Hamilton escape room, 167–172
  See also puzzles
codes and cyphers, 60, 77–78
The Codex, 6, 13–14
College of Wizardry LARP, 18–20
combat games, 118
conferences, escape rooms at, 35–36, 82, 92–102
Convention of Thorns, 19–20
corporations
  grants from, 31–32
  team-building by, 8, 80
counting, in puzzles, 81
critical thinking, 26, 80
Cross Roads Escape Games, 10
crossword puzzles, 60, 83, 161, 169–170
CSI: Library Murder Mystery room, 35–36*f*, 82
CSI: The Experience (Las Vegas), 14
curriculum support, 25–26
Curry, Jim, 51–52
cyphers and secret codes, 60, 77–78

D

debriefing, 68, 142
Deck Toys, 125, 132
decoders, 78–79, 137, 149–150
decorations and props, 68–69, 76, 84–85, 106–107, 123, 160–164, 173
DeFrain, Erica, 39–40
Demeter, 20
Denzer, Juan, 145–151
Dewey Decimal system games, 42–44, 57
Dewey Decimated program, 42–44
difficulty, levels of, 6–7, 91
digital breakouts, 125–132
directories, 179
Dodge City Public Library, 46–47
donations, 32
Dracula's Curse, 125–130

E

East Orange Public Library, 49–50, 119–124
Easter eggs, 84
education and teaching, 23–26, 147–148, 180
E-Exit Games, 13
electromagnetic locks, 81–82, 106, 160, 166, 172
Enchambered Live Escape Room Adventure, 10
endgame, deciding, 76–77
enthusiasts clubs, 103–109
Escape Code, 10
Escape Countdown, 6, 7*f*, 12, 80
Escape Dracula's Library program, 45
Escape Empire, 65
Escape Expert, 8
The Escape Game, 6, 11
Escape Reality, 12
Escape Room Nederland, 13
Escape Room: The Game, 136–137
escape rooms
  overview, ix–x, 3–9
  for children, 38–39, 49–50, 119–124
  designing from scratch, 71–86, 120–121

digital and online, 125–132
as educational tools, 23–26, 147–148
enthusiasts clubs for, 103–109
gameplay during, 9, 67–68, 85–86, 101–102
international rooms, 12–14
within larger events, 48–49
number of, ix, 3–4
partnerships with, 51–52, 90
pop-up rooms, 39–40, 89–102
pre-designed kits for, 23–24, 57–59, 63–69, 94–102, 141
for staff training, 25, 40–41, 139–143
start-to-finish model, 155–172
top-rated in the U.S., 10–12
types of, 5–6, 71–72
See also immersive experiences
Escape Rooms Portland, 35
Escape the Fairy Tale program, 49–50, 120–124
Escape the Room program, 47–48
Escape Thrill, 5*f*, 6, 12
An Evening in Paris room, 7*f*, 12
Exit game series, 137–138

F

Fairfield Public Library, 54–57
Fairweather Manor, 19
fairy tale-themed rooms, 49–50, 120–124
fandom experiences, x, 17–20, 59, 112
federal government, grants from, 31
The Ferguson Library, 54–57
flashlights, UV, 64, 69, 79, 81, 159–160, 171
Florida escape rooms, 6, 7, 11–12
Florida State College, 40–41, 139
flowcharts, 75–76
Flower Memorial Library, 37–38, 76
Follow the Maze puzzle, 148–149
forums and community groups, 180
foundations, grants from, 32
France, escape rooms in, 13
froth, defined, 28–29
funding and budgets, 30–33, 108–109

G

game-based learning, 23–26
gamemasters, 9, 100–101
gameplay, 9, 67–68, 85–86, 101–102
games, board, 65, 133–138
Germany, escape rooms and LARPs in, 6, 13, 18–20
"Getting Frothy" (Scherer), 27–29
Google Drawing, 128–131
Google Drive, 96, 99, 127–128, 130–131
Google Sites, 125–126, 130–131
government, grants from, 31
Gramm, Alec, 47–48
grants, 31–33, 108
grassroots fundraising, 32
Great Britain, escape rooms in, 12
group photos, 68, 102*f*

H

Hamilton escape room, 73–81, 155–172
Harry Potter experiences, x, 17–20, 59, 112
Heilman, Janice, 93–102
hidden messages, 78–79
hidden objects, 60, 79
high school escape rooms, 45, 53–54
hints and penalties, 85, 91
hotspots, 131
Howell Carnegie District Library, 93–102
Howitt, Grant, 28
HP Reveal, 114
Hungary, escape rooms in, 13
Husker History Mystery program, 39–40

I

images, objects in, 80
immersive experiences
hosting in libraries, 111–118
types of, 14–20
See also escape rooms
Improbable Escapes, 90
information literacy instruction, 25
Instructables.com, 77, 79, 109, 149–151
instruction sheets, 94, 98, 100
interactive museum exhibits, 14–16, 114
international escape rooms, 12–14

J

jigsaw puzzles, 60, 83, 128–129

K

Kansas escape rooms, 11
Kelly, Meagan, 132
kits, pre-designed, 23–24, 57–59, 63–69, 94–102, 141
Komnata Quest, 10

L

Lantz, Frank, 24
Laramie County Library System, 59
LARPs. *See* live action roleplaying (LARP)
Leap Motion, 146, 150
learning, game-based, 23–26
librarians
  contributions by, 27–29, 93–102, 114–118, 119–124, 145–153
  interviews with, 37–57
libraries
  budgets and funding, 30–33, 108–109
  case studies, 37–57
  escape rooms based on, 42–45, 57–59
  popular themes for escape rooms in, 60
  staff training for, 25, 40–41, 139–143
  STEM learning in, 23–24, 147–148
library advocacy, 27–29
library associations, grants from, 31
library conferences, 35–36, 82, 92–102
Library Lockdown program, 38–39
library orientation, 25, 58–59
Library Skills Save the Day program, 58–59
Lieberman, Marissa, 49–50, 119–124
light, use of, 64, 79, 81, 123, 159–160, 171
linear rooms and puzzles, 71–72, 168–172
littleBits, 147–148
live action roleplaying (LARP)
  in conjunction with escape rooms, 48–49
  directory of, 179
  examples of, x, 18–20
  hosting in libraries, 114–118
  as inspiration for escape rooms, 4
Lock Paper Scissors, 65, 120, 179
Locked in the Library game, 58
locks and lock kits
  from Breakout EDU, 30, 40, 64, 69, 99, 166
  digital and online, 126–127
  magnetic, 81–82, 106, 160, 166, 172
  putting together from scratch, 66, 81–82
"Look Mom, No Hands!" game, 150
Lopes, Melissa, 53–54

M

magnetic locks, 81–82, 106, 160, 166, 172
Maluck, Thomas, 52–53
Mannino, Tegan, 48–49, 114–118
marketing, 66–67, 104–105
Marvel Avengers S.T.A.T.I.O.N., 17
mazes, 39, 60, 148–149, 150, 152–153
McClure, Anna, 59
Michigan Library Association, 35, 82, 92–93
Missouri escape rooms, 10, 11
M&M Mastermind game, 94–102
mobile escape rooms, 39–40, 89–102
Monson Free Library, 48–49
Morning, Mackenzie, 41–42, 143
Morse code, 77–78, 149–150
Morton-James Public Library, 38–39, 106, 152–153
murder mysteries, 35, 115, 117
museum exhibits, interactive, 14–16, 114
Museum Heist program, 51–52
Museum of Modern Art, 14
Mystery at the Stargazer's Manor, 65, 135
Mythen, Susan, 40–41, 139–142

N

narratives, developing, 73, 120–121, 173
Nassau (NY) Library System, 27–29
National Library of Singapore, 4
National Museum of Singapore, 15
The Netherlands, escape rooms in, 13
New Orleans escape rooms, 11
New York escape rooms, 10

New York Law Institute, 16, 114
New York Public Library, 4
Nicholson, S., 79
nonlinear rooms and puzzles, 72, 157–159

O

objects
  hidden, 60, 79
  in images, 80
  used in an unusual way, 80
online breakouts, 125–132
orientation tours, 25, 58–59
O'Shaughnessy, Lisa, 49–50, 119–124
Our Senses exhibit, 15

P

Pace Gallery, 15
Page, Penny, 78*f*, 182
paintings, 78*f*, 80, 148, 158, 169, 182
Papaleka, Robin, 59
penalties and hints, 85, 91
Pennsylvania escape rooms, 5, 10
photos, post-game, 68, 102f
Pinterest boards, 65–66
pirate-themed rooms, 12, 13, 37–38, 60
players
  limiting the number of, 77
  statistics on, 7–8
pop-up escape rooms, 39–40, 89–102
pre-designed escape rooms, 23–24, 57–59, 63–69, 94–102, 141
pre-game experience, 67
props and decorations, 68–69, 76, 79–80, 84–85, 106–107, 123, 160–164, 173
public libraries. *See* libraries
Puzzled Pint code sheet, 77
puzzles
  in Alexander Hamilton escape room, 167–172
  designing, 74–75, 96–98
  linear, 71–72, 168–172
  nonlinear, 72, 157–159
  popular types of, 60, 77–84
  technology based, 147–153
  template for, 175–177
  websites for, 83–84

R

Rain Room, 14
rare books exhibit, AR in, 16, 114
Real Escape Game, 5, 12
research-based puzzles, 83
resetting, time frame for, 68
Richland Library, 52–53
riddles, 60, 81, 121–122
Roberts, Meghin, 37–38, 76
robots, 39, 150–153
Rochon, Emma, 90–92
Rogers-Whitehead, Carrie, 112
roleplaying, live. *See* live action roleplaying (LARP)
roleplaying games (RPGs), 117
Romania, escape rooms in, 6, 13–14
Room Escape Artist (blog), 4, 181
Room Escape Maker, 75, 132
rooms, escape. *See* escape rooms
Rubik's Cube, 151
Ruth Holder Public Library, 44–45

S

safety, 91–92
Salt Lake County Library, 112
scavenger hunts, 5, 72, 79, 113
Scherer, Nicole, 27–29, 54–57, 81, 83, 181
Sclippa, Eva, 42–44
The Search for Alexander Hamilton and the Missing Librarian, 73–81, 155–172
secret codes and cyphers, 60, 77–78
The Secret of Dr. Gravely's Retreat, 65, 134
set-up document template, 173–174
Ships of War puzzle, 78, 158, 161, 169
Signal-Book for the Ships of War (Edles), 78, 169
Singapore, events in, 4, 15
Skull and Crossbones, 20
Smith, Tara, 51–52
Smithsonian Museum, 14–15
Snap Circuits, 147–148
sound, in puzzles, 83
soundtracks, 84–85, 165
spell packets, 118
Sphero, 146, 150
Spina, Carli, 133
Spotify, 65, 85

Staff Development Day program, 40–41
staff training, 25, 40–41, 139–143
STEM and STEAM, 23–24, 106–107, 147–148

T

Tabletop Audio, 85, 116, 165
Tambasco, Brandi, 93–102
Tampa Bay Escape Room, 11
Teachers Pay Teachers, 83
teaching and education, 23–26, 147–148, 180
team-building, 8, 25, 40–41, 80, 139–143
teamLab: *Transcending Boundaries* exhibit, 15
technology, incorporating, 106–107, 113–114, 145–153
teens, escape rooms for, 44–45, 51–54
templates
- puzzle document, 175–177
- set-up document, 173–174

testing, beta, 85–86, 91, 132
themes
- conceptualizing, 72–73, 111–112
- popular, 60
- staying consistent with, 91

Thinkfun board games, 65, 134–135
Thoegersen, Jennifer, 38–40, 152–153
Thoegersen, Rasmus, 38–39, 152–153
Thomen, Rex, 26
Tippecanoe County Public Library, 47–48
Titanic-themed rooms, 10, 46–47
Treasures and Technology of the New York Law Institute, 16
troubleshooting, 68–69
"Twinkle, Twinkle, Little Star" puzzle, 149

U

United States
- first escape room in, 5
- number of escape rooms in, 4
- top escape rooms in, 10–12

University of Nebraska-Lincoln Libraries, 39–40
USA Today Best Escape Rooms list, 10–12
Use "The Force" maze, 150
UV flashlights, 64, 69, 79, 81, 159–160, 171

V

victory photos, 68, 102f

W

weapons, padded, 118
websites
- for blogs, 180–181
- for digital breakouts, 132
- for directories, 179
- for educational resources, 179
- for forums and community groups, 180
- for funding, 31–32, 108
- for puzzles, 83–84

The Werewolf Experiment game, 136
"Where's Waldo" puzzle, 148
Whitehead, April, 132
William Madison Randall Library, 42–44
Williams, Amy, 45
Windsor Locks Public Schools, 53–54
Winona State University Krueger Library, 41–42, 143
Wizard of Oz room, 46–47
The Wizarding World of Harry Potter, 17
The Wonderful World of Dewey game, 57

Y

Young Adult Library Services Association (YALSA), 31, 32, 108–109
YouTube, 85, 132, 149

Z

zombie-themed rooms, 37–38, 60